ON BECOMING A NOVELIST

THE HARPER & ROW SERIES ON THE PROFESSIONS

On Becoming a Novelist, *by John Gardner*
Growing Minds: On Becoming a Teacher, *by Herbert Kohl*

ON
BECOMING
A
NOVELIST

John Gardner

Foreword by Raymond Carver

Harper & Row, Publishers
New York, Cambridge, Philadelphia, San Francisco
London, Mexico City, São Paulo, Singapore, Sydney

For all my students

A hardcover edition of this book is published by Harper & Row, Publishers, Inc.

ON BECOMING A NOVELIST. Copyright © 1983 by the Estate of John Gardner. Foreword copyright © 1983 by Raymond Carver. All rights reserved. Printed in the United States of America. No part of this book may be used or reproduced in any manner whatsoever without written permission except in the case of brief quotations embodied in critical articles and reviews. For information address Harper & Row, Publishers, Inc., 10 East 53rd Street, New York, N.Y. 10022. Published simultaneously in Canada by Fitzhenry & Whiteside Limited, Toronto.

First HARPER COLOPHON edition published 1985.

Library of Congress Cataloging in Publication Data

Gardner, John, 1933–1982.
    On becoming a novelist.

    Includes index.
    1. Fiction—Authorship—Vocational guidance.
I. Title.
PN3365.G37 1983   808.3'023   82-48662
ISBN 0-06-014956-6
ISBN 0-06-091126-3 (pbk.)   86 87 88 MPC 6 5 4

CONTENTS

ACKNOWLEDGMENTS

Some of the plot ideas examined in this book came out of writers' workshop discussions at SUNY–Binghamton.

FOREWORD

A long time ago—it was the summer of 1958—my wife and I and our two baby children moved from Yakima, Washington, to a little town outside of Chico, California. There we found an old house and paid twenty-five dollars a month rent. In order to finance this move, I'd had to borrow a hundred and twenty-five dollars from a druggist I'd delivered prescriptions for, a man named Bill Barton.

This is by way of saying that in those days my wife and I were stone broke. We had to eke out a living, but the plan was that I would take classes at what was then called Chico State College. But for as far back as I can remember, long before we moved to California in search of a different life and our slice of the American pie, I'd wanted to be a writer. I wanted to write, and I wanted to write anything—fiction, of course, but also poetry, plays, scripts, articles for *Sports Afield*, *True*, *Argosy*, and *Rogue* (some of the magazines I was then reading), pieces for the local newspaper—anything that involved putting words together to make something coherent and of interest to someone besides myself. But at the time of our move, I felt in my bones I had to get some education in order to go along with being a writer. I put a very high premium on education then—much higher in those days than now, I'm sure, but that's because I'm older and have an education. Understand that nobody in my family had ever gone to college or for that matter had got beyond the mandatory eighth grade in high school. I didn't *know anything*, but I knew I didn't know anything.

So along with this desire to get an education, I had this very strong desire to write; it was a desire so strong that, with the encouragement I was given in college, and the insight acquired, I kept on writing long after "good sense" and the "cold facts"—the "realities" of my life told me, time and again, that I ought to quit, stop the dreaming, quietly go ahead and do something else.

That fall at Chico State I enrolled in classes that most freshman students have to take, but I enrolled as well for something called Creative Writing 101. This course was going to be taught by a new faculty member named John Gardner, who was already surrounded by a bit of mystery and romance. It was said that he'd taught previously at Oberlin College but had left there for some reason that wasn't made clear. One student said Gardner had been fired—students, like everyone else, thrive on rumor and intrigue—and another student said Gardner had simply quit after some kind of flap. Someone else said his teaching load at Oberlin, four or five classes of freshman English each semester, had been too heavy and that he couldn't find time to write. For it was said that Gardner was a real, that is to say a practicing, writer—someone who had written novels and short stories. In any case, he was going to teach CW 101 at Chico State, and I signed up.

I was excited about taking a course from a real writer. I'd never laid eyes on a writer before, and I was in awe. But where were these novels and short stories, I wanted to know. Well, nothing had been published yet. It was said that he couldn't get his work published and that he carried it around with him in boxes. (After I became his student, I was to see those boxes of manuscript. Gardner had become aware of my difficulty in finding a place to work. He knew I had a young family and

cramped quarters at home. He offered me the key to his office.
I see that gift now as a turning point. It was a gift not made
casually, and I took it, I think, as a kind of mandate—for that's
what it was. I spent part of every Saturday and Sunday in his
office, which is where he kept the boxes of manuscript. The
boxes were stacked up on the floor beside the desk. *Nickel
Mountain*, grease-pencilled on one of the boxes, is the only title
I recall. But it was in his office, within sight of his unpublished
books, that I undertook my first serious attempts at writing.)

When I met Gardner, he was behind a table at registration
in the women's gym. I signed the class roster and was given
a course card. He didn't look anywhere near what I imagined
a writer should look like. The truth is, in those days he looked
and dressed like a Presbyterian minister, or an FBI man. He
always wore a black suit, a white shirt, and a tie. And he had
a crewcut. (Most of the young men my age wore their hair in
what was called a "DA" style—a "duck's ass"—the hair
combed back along the sides of the head onto the nape and
plastered down with hair oil or cream.) I'm saying that Gardner looked very square. And to complete the picture he drove
a black four-door Chevrolet with black-wall tires, a car so
lacking in any of the amenities it didn't even have a car radio.
After I'd got to know him, had been given the key, and was
regularly using his office as a place to work, I'd be at his desk
in front of the window on a Sunday morning, pounding away
on his typewriter. But I'd be watching for his car to pull up
and park on the street out in front, as it always did every
Sunday. Then Gardner and his first wife, Joan, would get out
and, all dressed up in their dark, severe-looking clothes, walk
down the sidewalk to the church where they would go inside
and attend services. An hour and a half later I'd be watching
for them as they came out, walked back down the sidewalk to
their black car, got inside and drove away.

Gardner had a crewcut, dressed like a minister or an FBI
man, and went to church on Sundays. But he was unconven-

tional in other ways. He started breaking the *rules* on the first day of class; he was a chain smoker and he smoked continuously in the classroom, using a metal wastebasket for an ashtray. In those days, nobody smoked in a classroom. When another faculty member who used the same room reported on him, Gardner merely remarked to us on the man's pettiness and narrow-mindedness, opened windows, and went on smoking.

For short story writers in his class, the requirement was one story, ten to fifteen pages in length. For people who wanted to write a novel—I think there must have been one or two of these souls—a chapter of around twenty pages, along with an outline of the rest. The kicker was that this one short story, or the chapter of the novel, might have to be revised ten times in the course of the semester for Gardner to be satisfied with it. It was a basic tenet of his that a writer found what he wanted to say in the ongoing process of *seeing* what he'd said. And this seeing, or seeing more clearly, came about through revision. He *believed* in revision, endless revision; it was something very close to his heart and something he felt was vital for writers, at whatever stage of their development. And he never seemed to lose patience rereading a student story, even though he might have seen it in five previous incarnations.

I think his idea of a short story in 1958 was still pretty much his idea of a short story in 1982; it was something that had a recognizable beginning, middle, and an end to it. Once in a while he'd go to the blackboard and draw a diagram to illustrate a point he wanted to make about rising or falling emotion in a story—peaks, valleys, plateaus, resolution, *denouement*, things like that. Try as I might, I couldn't muster a great deal of interest or really understand this side of things, the stuff he put on the blackboard. But what I did understand was the way he would comment on a student story that was undergoing class discussion. Gardner might wonder aloud about the author's reasons for writing a story about a crippled person, say, and leaving out the fact of the character's crippledness until the very end of the story. "So you think it's a good idea not to let the reader know this man is crippled until the last sentence?" His tone of voice conveyed his disapproval, and it didn't take more than an instant for everyone in class, including the author of the story, to see that it wasn't a good strategy to use. Any strategy that kept important and necessary information away from the reader in the hope of overcoming him by surprise at the end of the story was cheating.

In class he was always referring to writers whose names I was not familiar with. Or if I knew their names, I'd never read the work. Conrad. Céline. Katherine Anne Porter. Isaac Babel. Walter van Tilburg Clark. Chekhov. Hortense Calisher. Curt Harnack. Robert Penn Warren. (We read a story of Warren's called "Blackberry Winter." For one reason or another, I didn't care for it, and I said so to Gardner. "You'd better read it again," he said, and he was not joking.) William Gass was another writer he mentioned. Gardner was just starting his magazine, *MSS*, and was about to publish "The Pedersen Kid" in the first issue. I began reading the story in manuscript, but I didn't understand it and again I complained to Gardner. This time he didn't tell me I should try it again, he simply took the story away from me. He talked about James Joyce and Flaubert and Isak Dinesen as if they lived just down the road, in Yuba City. He said, "I'm here to tell you who to read as well as teach you how to write." I'd leave class in a daze and make straight for the library to find books by these writers he was talking about.

Hemingway and Faulkner were the reigning authors in those days. But altogether I'd probably read at the most two or three books by these fellows. Anyway, they were so well-known and so much talked about, they couldn't be all that good, could they? I remember Gardner telling me, "Read all the Faulkner you can get your hands on, and then read all of Hemingway to clean the Faulkner out of your system."

He introduced us to the "little" or literary periodicals by bringing a box of these magazines to class one day and passing them around so that we could acquaint ourselves with their names, see what they looked like and what they felt like to hold in the hand. He told us that this was where most of the best fiction in the country and just about all of the poetry was appearing. Fiction, poetry, literary essays, book reviews of recent books, criticism of *living* authors *by* living authors. I felt wild with discovery in those days.

For the seven or eight of us who were in his class, he ordered heavy black binders and told us we should keep our written work in these. He kept his own work in such binders, he said, and of course that settled it for us. We carried our stories in those binders and felt we were special, exclusive, singled out from others. And so we were.

I don't know how Gardner might have been with other students when it came time to have conferences with them about their work. I suspect he gave everybody a good amount of attention. But it was and still is my impression that during that period he took my stories more seriously, read them closer and more carefully, than I had any right to expect. I was completely unprepared for the kind of criticism I received from him. Before our conference he would have marked up my story, crossing out unacceptable sentences, phrases, individual words, even some of the punctuation; and he gave me to understand that these deletions were not negotiable. In other cases he would bracket sentences, phrases, or individual words, and these were items we'd talk about, these cases were negotiable. And he wouldn't hesitate to add something to what I'd written —a word here and there, or else a few words, maybe a sentence that would make clear what I was trying to say. We'd discuss commas in my story as if nothing else in the world mattered more at that moment—and, indeed, it did not. He was always looking to find something to praise. When there was a sentence, a line of dialogue, or a narrative passage that he liked, something that he thought "worked" and moved the story along in some pleasant or unexpected way, he'd write "Nice" in the margin, or else "Good!" And seeing these comments, my heart would lift.

It was close, line-by-line criticism he was giving me, and the reasons behind the criticism, why something ought to be this way instead of that; and it was invaluable to me in my development as a writer. After this kind of detailed talk about the text, we'd talk about the larger concerns of the story, the "problem" it was trying to throw light on, the conflict it was trying to grapple with, and how the story might or might not fit into the grand scheme of story writing. It was his conviction that if the words in the story were blurred because of the author's insensitivity, carelessness, or sentimentality, then the story suffered from a tremendous handicap. But there was something even worse and something that must be avoided at all costs: if the words and the sentiments were dishonest, the author was faking it, writing about things he didn't care about or believe in, then nobody could ever care anything about it.

A writer's values and craft. This is what the man taught and what he stood for, and this is what I've kept by me in the years since that brief but all-important time.

This book of Gardner's seems to me to be a wise and honest assessment of what it is like and what is necessary to become a writer and stay a writer. It is informed by common sense, magnanimity, and a set of values that is not negotiable. Anyone reading it must be struck by the absolute and unyielding honesty of the author, as well as by his good humor and high-mindedness. Throughout the book, if you notice, the author keeps saying: "it has been my experience. . . ." It was his experience—and it has been mine, in my role as a teacher of creative writing—that certain aspects of writing can be taught and handed over to other, usually younger, writers. This idea shouldn't come as a surprise to any person seriously interested in education and the creative act. Most good or even great conductors, composers, microbiologists, ballerinas, mathematicians, visual artists, astronomers, or fighter pilots, learned their business from older and more accomplished practitioners. Taking classes in creative writing, like taking classes in pottery or medicine, won't in itself make anyone a great writer, potter, or doctor—it may not even make the person *good* at any of these things. But Gardner was convinced that it wouldn't hurt your chances, either.

One of the dangers in teaching or taking creative writing classes lies—and here I'm speaking from my experience again —in the overencouragement of young writers. But I learned from Gardner to take that risk rather than err on the other side. He gave and kept giving, even when the vital signs fluctuated wildly, as they do when someone is young and learning. A young writer certainly needs as much, I would even say more, encouragement than young people trying to enter other professions. And it ought to go without saying that the encouragement must always be honest encouragement and never hype. What makes this book particularly fine is the quality of its encouragement.

Failure and dashed hopes are common to us all. The suspicion that we're taking on water and that things are not working out in our life the way we'd planned hits most of us at some time or another. By the time you're nineteen you have a pretty good idea of some of the things you're *not* going to be; but more often, this sense of one's limitations, the really penetrating understanding, happens in late youth or early middle age. No teacher or any amount of education can make a writer out of someone who is constitutionally incapable of becoming a writer in the first place. But anyone embarking on a career, or pursuing a calling, risks setback and failure. There are failed policemen, politicians, generals, interior decorators, engineers, bus drivers, editors, literary agents, businessmen, basket weavers. There are also failed and disillusioned creative writing teachers and failed and disillusioned writers. John Gardner was neither of these, and the reasons why are to be found in this wonderful book.

My own debt is great and can only be touched on in this brief context. I miss him more than I can say. But I consider myself the luckiest of men to have had his criticism and his generous encouragement.

—RAYMOND CARVER

PREFACE

I assume that anyone looking at this preface to see whether or not it would perhaps be worthwhile to buy this book, or take it from the library, or steal it (don't), is doing so for one of two reasons. Either the reader is a beginning novelist who wants to know whether the book is likely to be helpful, or else the reader is a writing teacher hoping to figure out without too much wasted effort what kind of rip-off is being aimed this time at that favorite target of self-help fleecers. It's true that most books for beginning writers are not very good, even those written with the best of intentions, and no doubt this one, like others, will have its faults. Let me set down here how and why I've written it, and what I try to do.

After twenty-some years of giving readings and public lectures, along with making frequent visits to classes in creative writing, I have learned what questions to expect in the inevitable question-and-answer period—some questions at first glance merely polite ("Do you write with a pencil, a pen, or a typewriter?"); some professorial and freighted with vested interest ("Do you think it's important that the would-be novelist read widely in the classics?"); and some timid and serious, presented as if they were questions of life and death, which, for the person who asks them, they may well be, such as "How do I know if I'm really a writer?" This book puts together in one place my considered answers to the questions I take to be serious, including some questions I take to be more serious than they may sound to the casual ear. I answer each question directly but also discursively, trying to make sure I cover every aspect of the question, including those the questioner may have intended but didn't put in words. Some writers, I've found, make the general assumption that every question asked in an auditorium or a writing class is essentially frivolous, presented in order to draw attention to the asker, or to flatter the visitor and keep things rolling, or simply from mad whim. I try to err in the opposite direction. I assume, in classrooms and auditoriums, as elsewhere, that human beings are smarter and nobler than misanthropic souls imagine. I doubt that anyone whose interest in novel-writing is fake will bother to read this book, and I assume that anyone who cares deeply about writing will forgive me if I say, on any given subject, more than seems necessary, since he will sympathize with my purpose, which is to be useful and thorough.

Everything I say here is of course one writer's opinion—opinion grounded in years of writing, reading, teaching, editing, and arguing with my writer friends, but still only opinion, since art does not afford the testable certainties of geometry or physics. For that reason some of what I say will undoubtedly be, for some readers, off the mark or even offensive. On some subjects—for instance, writers' workshops—one is tempted to pull punches or rest satisfied with oversimplified answers; but I'm assuming, as the primary reader of this book, an intensely serious beginning novelist who wants the strict truth (as I perceive it) for his life's sake, so that he can plan his days and years in ways beneficial to his art; avoid false paths of technique, theory, and attitude; and become as quickly and efficiently as possible a master of his craft.

This book is elitist, in a sense. I do not mean that I write mainly for that very special novelist who desires only a small coterie of intensely sophisticated, well-educated, and subtle readers, though to that writer I would recommend this book, both as an aid and as an argument for humane moderation. The elitism I mean is more temperate and middle class. I write for those who desire, not publication at any cost, but publication one can be proud of—serious, honest fiction, the kind of novel that readers will find they enjoy reading more than once, the kind of fiction likely to survive. Fine workmanship—art that avoids cheap and easy effects, takes no shortcuts, struggles never to lie even about the most trifling matters (such as which object, precisely, an angry man might pick up to throw at his kitchen wall, or whether a given character would in fact say "you aren't" or the faintly more assertive "you're not")—workmanship, in short, that impresses us partly by its painstaking care, gives pleasure and a sense of life's worth and dignity not only to the reader but to the writer as well. This book is for the beginning novelist who has already figured out that it is far more satisfying to write well than simply to write well enough to get published.

This is not essentially a book on craft, though here and there I give what some may find valuable pointers. It's not that I disapprove of books on craft or believe no good book of the kind can be written—in fact, I've written such a book myself and use it with my students, changing and expanding it year by year, with the expectation that sooner or later it will seem to me worth making public. But the object of the present book is more grand and more humble: I try here to deal with, and if possible get rid of, the beginning novelist's worries.

Trying to help the beginning writer overcome his worries may at first seem a rather foolish project; my memory of my own apprentice years and my experience with other beginning writers suggest that it's not. The whole world seems to conspire against the young novelist. The young man or woman who announces an intention of becoming an M.D. or an electrical engineer or a forest ranger is not immediately bombarded with well-meant explanations of why the ambition is impractical, out of reach, a waste of time and intelligence. "Go ahead, try it," we say, secretly thinking: If he can't make the grade as an M.D., he can always become an osteopath. Writing teachers, on the other hand, and books about writing, not to mention friends, relatives, and professional writers, are quick to point out the terrible odds (thereby increasing them) against anyone's (ever, anywhere) becoming a successful writer. "Writing takes a rare and special gift," they say (not strictly true); "The market for writing gets worse every year" (largely false); or, "You'll starve!" (maybe so). And the discouragement offered by other human beings is the least of it. Writing a novel takes an immense amount of time, at least for most people, and can test the writer's psyche beyond endurance. The writer asks himself day after day, year after year, if he's fooling himself, asks why people write novels anyhow—long, careful studies of the hopes, joys, and disasters of creatures who, strictly speaking, do not exist. The writer may be undermined by creeping misanthropy, while the writer's wife, or husband, is growing sulky and embarrassed. The idiots who write for TV pull in money by the fistful, while this saint among mortals, the novelist, pumps gas, types memos, or sells life insurance to keep food in the mouths of his children. Or the writer may slide into alcoholism, the number one occupational hazard of the trade.

Almost no one mentions that for a certain kind of person nothing is more joyful or satisfying than the life of a novelist, if not for its financial rewards then for others; that one need not turn into a misanthrope or a drunk; that in fact one can be a more or less successful M.D., engineer, or forest ranger, even follow the unfashionable profession of housewife, and *also* be a novelist—at any rate, many novelists, both great and ordinary, have done it. This book tries to give honest reassurance by making plain what the life of a novelist is like; what the novelist needs to guard against, inside himself and outside; what he can reasonably expect and what, in general, he cannot. It is a book that celebrates novel-writing and encourages the reader to give it a try if he or she is seriously so inclined. The worst that can happen to the writer who tries and fails—unless he has inflated or mystical notions of what it is to be a novelist —is that he will discover that, for him, writing is not the best place to seek joy and satisfaction. More people fail at becoming successful businessmen than fail at becoming artists.

I.

THE WRITER'S
NATURE

Nearly every beginning writer sooner or later asks (or wishes he dared ask) his creative writing teacher, or someone else he thinks might know, whether or not he really has what it takes to be a writer. The honest answer is almost always, "God only knows." Occasionally the answer is, "Definitely yes, if you don't get sidetracked," and now and then the answer is, or should be, "I don't think so." No one who's taught writing for very long, or has known many beginning writers, is likely to offer an answer more definite than one of these, though the question becomes easier to answer if the would-be writer means not just "someone who can get published" but "a serious novelist," that is, a dedicated, uncompromising artist, and not just someone who can publish a story now and then—in other words, if the beginning writer is the kind of person this book is mainly written for.

The truth is that there are so many magazines in the United States—not to speak of all those elsewhere—that almost anyone, if he's stubborn enough, can sooner or later get a story published; and once the beginning writer has been published in one magazine (some obscure quarterly, let us say), so that he can say in his covering letter to other editors, "Previous fiction of mine has appeared in such and such a journal," the better his chances are of reaching publication in other magazines. Success breeds success. For one thing, publication in five or six obscure magazines virtually guarantees eventual success in some not so obscure magazine, because editors, when in doubt, tend to be swayed by a record of publication elsewhere. And for another thing, the more the beginning writer writes and publishes (especially when he publishes after an exchange of letters with an intelligent editor willing to give advice), the more confident and proficient the beginning writer becomes. As for getting a not very good novel published, the possibilities are richer than one might think—though the pay may not be good. There are always publishers looking for new talent and willing to take risks, including a good number of publishers actively seeking bad fiction (pornography, horror novels, and so forth). Some young writers, by a quirk of their nature, cannot feel they are really writers until they have published somewhere, *any*where. Such writers are probably wise to do it and get it over with, though they'd be wiser yet to improve their skills and publish somewhere better, for the future's sake. It's hard to live down one's shoddy publications, and it's hard to scrap cheap techniques once they've worked. It's like trying to stop cheating at marriage or golf.

To answer the serious young writer's question responsibly, the writing teacher, or whoever, needs to consider a variety of indicators, none of them sure but each of them offering a useful hint. Some of these have to do with visible or potential ability, some with character. The reason none of the indicators is foolproof is partly that they're relative, and partly that the writer can improve—changing old habits of technique or personality, getting better by stubborn determination—or simply grow at a later stage from a probable nonwriter to a probable success.

1

One might begin the list anywhere; for convenience, let me begin with verbal sensitivity.

Good grades in English may or may not go with verbal sensitivity, that is, with the writer's gift for, and interest in, understanding how language works. Good grades in English may have more to do with the relative competence, sensitivity, and sophistication of the teacher than with the student writer's ability. It is not quite true to say that every good writer has a keen feeling for sentence rhythms—the music of language— or for the connotations and diction levels (domains) of words. Some great writers are great in spite of occasional lapses— clunky sentences, feeble metaphors, even foolish word choices. Theodore Dreiser can write: "He found her extremely intel- lectually interesting"—language so cacophonous and dull most good writers would run from it; yet few readers would deny that Dreiser's *Sister Carrie* and *An American Tragedy* are works of art. The writer with a tin ear, if he's good enough at other things, may in the end write deeper, finer novels than the most eloquent verbal musician.

And it must be added that the true artist's verbal sensitivity may be something the ordinary English teacher, or even the most sophisticated user of language, may fail to recognize at first glance. Many people who care a good deal about language are horrified, for instance, to hear "hopefully" used in the sense "it is hoped," or to hear politicians say "forthcoming" when they mean "forthright," or businesspeople say "feedback" when they mean "reaction" or "response"; and given this dis- taste for linguistic change, or perhaps distaste for certain classes of humanity, the sophisticated stickler may dismiss without thought an ingenious and sensitive use of the suspect word or phrase. The true artist's verbal sensitivity may well be differ- ent, in other words, from that of the usual "writer of good English." Black street kids playing "The Dozens"—piling up ingenious metaphorical insults of one another's mothers, not all of the metaphors grammatical or unmixed—may in fact be showing more verbal sensitivity than the speechwriters who helped create the image of John Kennedy. Moreover, as the example of Dreiser perhaps suggests, not every kind of writer requires the same measure of verbal sensitivity. A poet, to practice his art with success, must have an ear for language so finely tuned and persnickety as to seem to the ordinary novelist almost diseased. The short story writer, since the emotional charge of his fiction must reveal itself quickly, has a similar need for lyrical compression, though a need less desperate than the poet's. In the novelist, a hypersensitive ear may occasionally prove a handicap.

But though some great writers may at times write awkwardly, it is nevertheless the case that one sign of the born writer is his gift for finding or (sometimes) inventing authentically interesting language. His sentence rhythms fit what he is saying, rushing along when the story rushes, turning somewhat ponderous to deal with a ponderous character, echoing the thunder of which the story tells, or capturing aurally the wobble of the drunk, the slow, dull pace of the tired old man, the touching silliness of the forty-year-old woman who flirts. The writer sensitive to language finds his own metaphors, not simply because he has been taught to avoid clichés but because he enjoys finding an exact and vivid metaphor, one never before thought of, so far as he knows. If he uses an odd word, it is never the fashionable odd word of his time and place—for instance (as of this writing), "ubiquitous," or "detritus," or "serendipitous"—he uses his *own* odd word, not solely because he wants to be noticed as original (though that is likely to be part of it) but also because he's fascinated by words. He's interested in discovering the secrets words carry, whether or not he ever puts them in his fiction—for instance, how "discover" means "to take the cover off." He's interested in playing with sentence formation, seeing how long he can make a sentence go, or how many short sentences he can use without the reader's noticing. In short, one sign of a writer's potential is his especially sharp ear—and eye—for language.

If once in a while the beginning writer does something interesting with language—shows that he's actually listening to himself and looking closely at words, spying out their secrets—that is sign enough of the writer's promise. Only a talent that doesn't exist at all can't be improved. Usually. On the other hand, if as readers we begin to suspect that the writer cares about nothing *but* language, we begin to worry that he may be in for trouble. Normal people, people who haven't been misled by a faulty college education, do not read novels for words alone. They open a novel with the expectation of finding a story, hopefully with interesting characters in it, possibly an interesting landscape here and there, and, with any luck at all, an idea or two—with real luck a large and interesting cargo of ideas. Though there are exceptions, as a rule the good novelist does not worry primarily about linguistic brilliance—at least not brilliance of the showy, immediately obvious kind—but instead worries about telling his story in a moving way, making the reader laugh or cry or endure suspense, whatever it is that this particular story, told at its best, will incline the reader to do.

We read five words on the first page of a really good novel and we begin to forget that we are reading printed words on a page; we begin to see images—a dog hunting through garbage cans, a plane circling above Alaskan mountains, an old lady furtively licking her napkin at a party. We slip into a dream, forgetting the room we're sitting in, forgetting it's lunchtime or time to go to work. We recreate, with minor and for the most part unimportant changes, the vivid and continuous dream the writer worked out in his mind (revising and revising until he got it right) and captured in language so that other human beings, whenever they feel like it, may open his book and dream that dream again. If the dream is to be *vivid*, the writer's "language signals"—his words, rhythms, metaphors, and so on—must be sharp and sufficient: if they're vague, careless, blurry, or if there aren't enough of them to let us see clearly what is being presented, then the dream as we dream it will be cloudy, confusing, ultimately annoying and boring. And if the dream is to be *continuous,* we must not be roughly jerked from the dream back to the words on the page by language that's distracting. Thus, for example, if the writer makes some grammatical mistake, the reader stops thinking about the old lady at the party and looks, instead, at the words on the page, seeing if the sentence really is, as it seems, ungrammatical. If it is, the reader thinks about the writer, or possibly about the editor—"How come they let him get away with a thing like that?"—not about the old lady whose story has been interrupted.

The writer who cares more about words than about story (characters, action, setting, atmosphere) is unlikely to create a vivid and continuous dream; he gets in his own way too much; in his poetic drunkenness, he can't tell the cart—and its cargo —from the horse. So in judging the young writer's verbal sensitivity one does not ask only, "Has he got any?" but also, "Has he got too much?" If he has none, he's in for trouble, though as I've said, he may succeed anyway, either because he has something else that compensates for the weakness, or because, once the weakness has been pointed out, he's able to learn. If the writer has too much verbal sensitivity, his success —if he means to write novels, not poems—will depend (1) on his learning to care about other elements of fiction, so that, for their sake, he holds himself back a little, like a compulsive punster at a funeral, or (2) on his finding an editor and a body of readers who love, beyond all else, the same thing he loves, fine language. Such editors and readers do appear from time to time, refined spirits devoted to an exquisitely classy game we call fiction only by stretching the term to the breaking point.

The writer who cares chiefly or exclusively about language is poorly equipped for novel-writing in the usual sense because his character and personality are wrong for writing novels. By "character" I mean here what is sometimes called the individual's "inscribed" nature, his innate self; by "personality" I mean the sum of his typical and habitual ways of relating to those around him. I mean to distinguish, in other words, between the inner and outer selves. Those who inordinately love words as words are of a character type distinct enough, at least in broad outline, to be recognizable almost at a glance. Words seem inevitably to distance us from the brute existents (real trees, stones, yawling babies) that words symbolize and, in our thought processes, tend to replace. At any rate, so philosophers like Hobbes, Nietzsche, and Heidegger have maintained, and our experience with punsters seems to confirm the opinion. When a man makes a pun in a social situation, no one present can doubt—however we may admire the punster and the pun —that the punster has momentarily drawn back, disengaging himself, making connections he could not think of if he were fully involved in the social moment. For example, if we are admiring the art treasures of a family named Cheuse and the punster remarks, "Beggars can't be Cheuses!" we know at once that the punster is not peering deeply and admiringly into the Turner landscape at hand. The person profoundly in love with words may make an excellent poet, composer of crossword puzzles, or Scrabble player; he may write novel-like things which a select group admires; but he will probably not in the end prove a first-rate novelist.

For several reasons (first, because of his personality, which keeps the world of brute existence at arm's length), he is not likely to feel passionate attachment to the ordinary, mainstream novel. The novel's unashamed engagement with the world—the myriad details that make character come alive, the sustained fascination with the gossip surrounding the lives of imaginary beings, the naive emphasis on what happened next and what, precisely, the weather was that day—all these are likely to seem, to the word fanatic, silly and tedious; he feels himself buried in litter. And no one is much inclined to spend days, weeks, years, imitating an existence he does not really like in the first place. The word fanatic may love certain very special, highly intellectual novelists (Stendhal, Flaubert,

Robbe-Grillet, the Joyce of *Finnegans Wake*, possibly Nabokov), but he is likely to admire only for their secondary qualities novelists whose chief strength is the hurly-burly of vividly imitated reality (Dickens, Stevenson, Tolstoy, Melville, Bellow). I do not mean that the person primarily interested in linguistic artifice is blocked from all appreciation of good books whose main appeal comes from character and action; nor do I mean that, because by nature he distances himself from actuality, he is too icy of heart to love his wife and children. I mean only that his admiration of the mainstream novel is not likely to be sufficient to drive him to extend the tradition. If he's lucky enough to live in an aristocratic age, or if he can find the sanctuary of an aesthetic coterie—a walled enclave from which the great, fly-switching herd of humanity is excluded— the artificer may be able to work his quirky wonders. In a democratic age served largely by commercial publishers, only extraordinary ego and stubbornness can keep him going. We may all agree (and then again we may not) that the specialized fiction he writes is worthwhile; but to the extent that he suspects that his time and place are unworthy of his genius, to the extent that he feels detached from the concerns of the herd, or feels that his ideal is either meaningless or invisible to most of humanity, his will is undermined. Not caring much about the kind of novel most experienced and well-educated readers like to read, and not deeply in love with his special coterie—since ironic distance is part of his nature, perhaps even deep, misanthropic distrust like Flaubert's—he manages to bring out, in his lifetime, only one or two books. Or none.

By virtue of his personality—in the special sense in which I'm using that word—the brilliant artificer's novel is likely to suffer one of two harsh fates: either it never gets written at all (an excellent way of expressing one's scorn for one's audience and its interests) or it is spoiled by sentimentality, mannerism, or frigidity.

To publish a work of novel length, one must find, as I've

said, a coterie or else find some means of satisfying the ordinary reader's first requirement for any piece of writing longer than fifteen pages, namely profluence—the sense that things are moving, getting somewhere, flowing forward. The common reader demands some reason to keep turning the pages. Two things can keep the common reader going, argument or story. (Both are always involved, however subtly, in good fiction.) If an argument just keeps saying the same thing, never progressing from *a* to *b,* or if a story seems to be moving nowhere, the reader loses interest. To put it another way, if the reader finds nothing to feel suspense about (Where is this argument leading? or, What will happen if the rationalistic philosopher begins to believe in the warnings of his psychic student?), he eventually puts down the book. Every writer knows, in his bones if not elsewhere, that the vast majority of readers expects some kind of progress in a book (even if, according to some theory the writer holds, they are wrong to expect it), and the writer who sets out to do what he knows most of his readers don't want him to do—the writer who refuses to tell a story or advance an argument—is likely to find, sooner or later, that he simply cannot go on. Spending a lifetime writing novels is hard enough to justify in any case, but spending a lifetime writing novels nobody wants is much harder. If ten or twelve critics praise one's work and the rest of the world ignores it, it is hard to keep up one's conviction that the friendly critics are not crackpots. This is not to say that the serious writer should try to write for everyone—try to win the audience both of Saul Bellow and of Stephen King. But if one tries to write for nobody, only for some pure and unearthly ideal of aesthetic perfection, one is apt to lose heart.

Needless to say, most writers who care immoderately about language don't go to the extreme of refusing to tell a story at all. More commonly such writers do present characters, actions, and the rest, but becloud them in a mist of beautiful noise, forever getting in the way of *what* they are saying by the splendor of their way of saying it. Eventually one begins to suspect that the writer cares more about his gift than about his characters. Granted, the suspicion may be wrong. I think no fair-minded reader can doubt that in the fiction of Dylan Thomas the fundamental impulse is to capture real life, the special quality of country-Welsh craziness. Yet it's the metaphors, the slam-cram poetry we remember, not so much the people. Or think of John Updike. The brilliant language with which he describes a minor character cannot help but suggest that the words he chooses are more important to him than the token secretary behind the desk.

It is true that one of the pleasures afforded by good books is the writer's fine handling of language. But the dazzling poetry of Mercutio's Queen Mab speech is not the same poetry Hamlet speaks, while Hamlet's murderer-stepfather Claudius favors dull pentameters. Shakespeare fits language to its speaker and occasion, as the best writers always do. Both Hamlet and Mercutio are in some sense unbalanced, but the difference between the two kinds of imbalance is marked. Mercutio's madness is fantastic and phantasmic; Hamlet's is the madness of diseased irony and constraint. Mercutio flails and howls, piling metaphor on metaphor; Hamlet is so subtle in his neurotic meanness that his enemies often don't know they've been insulted. For instance, when his stepfather has asked him to adjust, be reasonable, stop wearing mourning clothes and harping on his father's death, be a dutiful citizen, Hamlet answers, "I'll serve you in my best." In the old medieval sense, "in my best" means "in black," in other words, in mourning clothes. He is saying, in the sly way of the hostile neurotic, both "I will do as you say" and "I defy you." In the work of Shakespeare, brilliant language always serves character and action. However splendid it may be, Shakespeare's language is finally subservient to character and plot.

If a writer cares more for his language than for other elements of fiction, if he continually calls our attention away from the story to himself, we call him "mannered" and eventually we tire of him. (Smart editors tire of him quickly and reject him.) If the writer seems to have less feeling for his characters than we feel they deserve, insofar as they reflect actual humanity, we call the writer "frigid." If he fakes feeling, or appears to do so—especially if he tries to achieve sentiment by cheap, dishonest means (for instance, by substituting language, "rhetoric," for authentically moving events)—we call him "sentimental."

So one of the things one considers when asked if the young writer has what it takes to become a good novelist is his feeling for language. If he's capable of writing expressively, at least sometimes, and if his love for language is not so exclusive or obsessive as to rule out all other interests, one feels the young writer has a chance. The better the writer's feel for language and its limits, the better his odds become. They are very good indeed for the writer who has a fine ear for language and *also* a fascination with the materials—character, action, setting— that make up fictional realities. He may develop into the virtuoso stylist (Proust, the later Henry James, or Faulkner) who has the best of both worlds.

The writer with the worst odds—the person to whom one at once says, "I don't think so"—is the writer whose feel for language seems incorrigibly perverted. The most obvious example is the writer who cannot move without the help of such phrases as "with a merry twinkle in her eye," or "the adorable twins," or "his hearty, booming laugh"—dead expressions, the cranked-up zombie emotion of a writer who feels nothing in his daily life or nothing he trusts enough to find his own words for, so that he turns instead to "she stifled a sob," "friendly lopsided smile," "cocking an eyebrow in that quizzical way he had," "his broad shoulders," "his encircling arm," "a faint smile curving her lips," "his voice was husky," "her face framed by auburn curls."

The trouble with such language is not only that it is cliché (worn out, overused); but also that it is symptomatic of a crippling psychological set. We all develop linguistic masks (arrays of verbal habits) with which to deal with the world; different masks for different occasions. And one of the most successful masks known, at least for dealing with troublesome situations, is the Christian Pollyanna mask embodied and atrophied in phrases like those I've mentioned. Why the mask turns up more often in writing than in normal speaking—why, that is, the art of writing becomes a way of prettifying and tranquilizing reality—I cannot say, unless it has to do with how writing is taught, in our early years, as a form of good manners, and also perhaps with the emphasis our first teachers give to the goody-goody (or taming) emotions fashionable in school readers. In any event, the Pollyanna mask, if it cannot be torn off, will spell ruin for the novelist. People who regularly seek to feel the bland optimism the Pollyanna mask supports cannot help developing a vested interest in seeing, speaking, and feeling as they do—with two results: they lose the power to see accurately, and they lose the power to communicate with any but those who see and feel in the same benevolently distorted way. Once one has made a strong psychological investment in a certain kind of language, one has trouble understanding that it distorts reality, and also trouble understanding how others—in this case those who take a more cautious or warily ironic view—can be so blind. No one with a distorted view of reality can write good novels, because as we read we measure fictional worlds against the real world. Fiction elaborated out of attitudes we find childish or tiresome in life very soon becomes tiresome.

The Pollyanna mask is only one among many common evasions of reality. Consider a few lines by a well-known science fiction writer:

It's not often people will tell you how they *really* feel about gut-level things. Like god or how they're afraid they'll go insane like their grandfather or sex or how obnoxious you are when you pick your nose and wipe it on your pants. They play cozy with you, because nobody likes to be hated, and large doses of truth from any one mouth tend to make the wearer of the mouth *persona non grata*. Particularly if he's caught you picking your nose and wiping it on your pants. Even worse if he catches you eating it.*

This is not the Pollyanna style favored by hack writers of the twenties and thirties but the hack-writer style that superseded it, disPollyanna. Sunny optimism, with its fondness for italics, gives way to an ill-founded cynicism, also supported by italics ("It's not often people will tell you how they *really* feel"), and "broad shoulders" give way to "gut-level things," or worse. Sentence fragments become common (a standard means of falsely heightening the emotion of what one says), and commas disappear ("grandfather or sex or how obnoxious you are") in rhetorical imitation of William Faulkner, who was also on thin ice. (Dropping commas is all right except if one's purpose is to increase the rush of the sentence and thus suggest emotion not justified by what is being said.) Instead of giving "friendly lopsided smiles" people "play cozy with you," which means that they're false, unreal, not even the owners (just the wearers) of their mouths. (The same stock depersonalization of human beings gives cheap detective fiction one of its favorite rhetorical devices, the transformation of "the man in the gray suit" to "Gray Suit," and the man in the sharkskin to "Sharkskin," as in "Gray Suit looks over at Sharkskin. 'Piss off,' he says." This tends to happen even in fairly good detective fiction. It's hard to rise above your class.) Crude jokes and images, slang phrases borrowed from foreign languages, are all stock in disPollyanna fiction—in an attempt to shock prudes. No one is shocked, of course, though a few may misread their annoyance as shock. One is annoyed because the whole thing is phony, an imitation of things too often imitated before. The problem with such

*Harlan Ellison, *Over the Edge* (New York: Belmont Books, 1970), p. 18.

writers, it ought to be mentioned, is not that they are worse people than those who wrote in Pollyanna. They are almost exactly the same people: idealists, people who simple-mindedly long for goodness, justice, and sanity; the difference is one of style. This same science fiction writer's character Jack the Ripper reacts in howling moral outrage when he learns how the Utopians have made him their plaything:

> A psychopath, a butcher, a lecher, a hypocrite, a clown.
> "You did this to me! Why did you do this?"
> Frenzy cloaked his words. . . .*

A young writer firmly hooked on bad science fiction, or the worst of the hard-boiled detective school, or tell-it-like-it-is so-called serious fiction, fashionably interpreting all experience as crap, may get published, if he works hard, but the odds are that he'll never be an artist. That may not bother him much. Hack writers are sometimes quite successful, even admired. But so far as I can see, they are of slight value to humanity.

Both Pollyanna and disPollyanna limit the writer in the same ways, leading him to miss and simplify experience, and cutting him off from all but fellow believers. Marxist language can have the same effects, or the argot of the ashram, or computer talk ("input"), or the weary metaphors of the business-and-law world ("where the cheese starts to bind"). When one runs across a student whose whole way of seeing and whose emotional security seem dependent on adherence to a given style of language, one has reason to worry.

Yet even linguistic rigidity of the kind I've been discussing is no sure sign of doom. Though some would-be writers may be incurably addicted to a particular way of oversimplifying language, others who seem no better off prove curable, once they've understood the problem and worked on it. What the writer must do to cure himself is rise above his own acquired bad taste, figure out how his language habits are like and unlike

*Over the Edge, p. 96.

the language habits of other people, and learn to recognize the relative virtues (and limitations) of language styles surrounding his own. This may mean working closely with a teacher who is sensitive to language, not only "good English" in the sense of "standard English," but vivid, expressive English, "standard" or not. Or it may mean thinking hard about words, phrases, sentence structure, rhythm, and the like; reading books about language; and above all, reading the work of universally acclaimed literary artists.

Every word and phrase, from holy to clinical to obscene, has its proper domain, where it works effectively and comfortably, offending no one. For instance, the phrase "We are gathered this day" is hardly noticeable floating from a pulpit, sounds ironic coming from a professor in a classroom, and in a business letter may sound insane. A phrase like "the blond youth" may be all but invisible in the foliage of an old-time novel but stands out in a modern one written in colloquial style. A comic vision of culture may help: the recognition that all human beings and literary styles have their amusing imperfections—the tendency of people and their language to slip into puffed-up pride, fake humility, dumb cunning, pretentious or fake-unpretentious intelligence. If all human styles are prone to reflect our human clownishness, we need not view any style with superstitious awe nor dismiss any style out of hand. We need only to figure out exactly what it is that we're trying to say—partly by saying it and then by looking it over to see if it says what we really mean—and to keep fiddling with the language until whatever objections we may consider raising seem to fall away.

To put all this more philosophically, language inevitably carries values with it, and unexamined language carries values one might, if one knew they were there, be ashamed of accidentally promoting. People sensitive to the disadvantage placed on women in our culture are likely to be annoyed each time common English usage makes us say "man" or "men" or "mankind" when we really mean "people"—or "he," as I mostly do (not that I like it) when I am speaking of the writer, whoever he or she may be. All of us are to some extent tricked by our language, thinking of the brain in terms of telephone circuits, or of the sun as "rising," or of "discovery" as (in faintly Platonic fashion) the uncovering of something that was always there ("He discovered a new way of eliminating fumes"). But the writer excessively tricked by language, "stuck" in the norms and prejudices of some narrow community, or unable to shake the influence and vision of some literary model—Faulkner or Joyce or the common locutions of bad science fiction—will never be a writer of the first rank because he will never be able to see clearly for himself.

The writer who knows himself to be insufficiently sensitive to language might try some of the following:

Get a first-rate freshman composition book (the best, in my opinion, is W. W. Watt's *An American Rhetoric*) and work hard, with or without a teacher, on everything you're unsure of, especially those sections dealing with style, diction, and sentence structure.

Create and work hard on exercises of your own. For example:

—Write an authentic sentence four pages long (do not cheat by using colons and semicolons that are really periods).

—Write a two- or three-page passage of successful prose (that is, prose that's not annoying or distracting) entirely in short sentences.

—Write a brief incident in five completely different styles—such an incident as: A man gets off a bus, stumbles, looks over and sees a woman, smiling.

Improve your vocabulary, not in the *Reader's Digest* way (which encourages the use of fashionable big words) but by systematically copying from your dictionary all the relatively short, relatively common words that you would not ordinarily think to use, with definitions if necessary, and then making an effort to use them as if they'd come to you naturally—use them, in other words, as naturally and casually as you'd use words at a party.

Read books and magazines, paying careful attention to the language. If what you're reading is bad (you can generally count on women's magazine fiction), underline or highlight the words and phrases that annoy you by their triteness, cuteness, sentimentality, or whatever—in other words, anything that would distract an intelligent, sensitive reader from the vivid and continuous dream. If what you are reading is good (you can usually count on *The New Yorker*, at least for diction), account for why the language succeeds. Perhaps even type out a masterpiece such as James Joyce's "The Dead."

If the promising writer keeps on writing—writes day after day, month after month—and if he reads very carefully, he will begin to "catch on." Catching on is important in the arts, as in athletics. Practical sciences, including the verbal engineering of commercial fiction, can be taught and learned. The arts too can be taught, up to a point; but except for certain matters of technique, one does not learn the arts, one simply catches on.

If my own experience is representative, what one mainly catches on to is the value of painstaking—almost ridiculously painstaking—work. I'd been writing happily since the age of eight, the age at which I first discovered the joys of doggerel; I'd written poems, stories, novels, and plays in high school; in college and graduate school I'd taken good courses in understanding fiction and good creative writing courses, some with well-known writers and editors, and I'd worked with real devotion through the other sorts of courses one takes to get a PhD; but somehow, for all that, I wasn't very good. I worked more hours at my fiction than anyone else I knew, and I was lavishly praised by friends and teachers, even published a little;

but I was dissatisfied, and I knew my dissatisfaction was not just churlishness. The study where I buried myself alive, the first year or two after graduate school (a toolshed so small I could touch the outer walls from the center, and so poorly ventilated that the smoke of my pipe made my typewriter vanish in fog), came to be so crammed with my manuscripts and drafts that I couldn't move my chair—yet still nothing I wrote seemed worth the trouble.

I had by this time already faced the painful truth every committed young writer must eventually face, that he's on his own. Teachers and editors may give bits of good advice, but they usually do not care as much as does the writer himself about his future, and they are far from infallible; in fact, I am convinced, after years of teaching and editing, and watching others do the same, that a large sample of comments by teachers and editors, myself included, would show these comments to be more often wrong, for the particular writer, than right. I, at any rate, had worked with teachers generally considered outstanding, had done my best at the young writers' hothouse, the Iowa Workshop, and had weaseled whatever help I could get out of other writers I admired. But now nothing was clearer than that I must figure out on my own what was wrong with my fiction.

Then I fell into an odd piece of luck. In conversation with a slightly older colleague at the California State University, Chico, where I was teaching at the time, I suggested that the two of us do an anthology of fiction including (as anthologies did not then do and most anthologies do not do now) not only short stories but also other forms—fables, tales, yarns, sketches, etc. The result was *The Forms of Fiction,* a book (now long out of print and almost impossible to get hold of) that provided a close analysis of the narratives we included. A more important result, for me, was that I learned about taking pains. Lennis Dunlap, my collaborator, was and remains one of the most infuriatingly stubborn perfectionists I have ever known. Night after night for two full years we would work for five, six, seven hours on what sometimes added up to three or four sentences. He drove me crazy, and he wasn't so kind to himself, either: often we had to stop because the stress of working with a young man as impatient as I was would give Lennis a histamine headache. Gradually I came to feel as unwilling as he was to let a sentence stand if the meaning was not as unambiguously visible as a grizzly bear in a brightly lit kitchen. I discovered what every good writer knows, that getting down one's exact meaning helps one to discover what one means. Looking back now at our writing in *The Forms of Fiction*, I find the style overly cautious, a bit too tight. (Sometimes saying a thing twice is a good idea.) But that painful two years—the midnight fights and sometimes the shock of joy we would both experience when the right choice of words made us grasp the idea that had until that instant teased and eluded us—showed me what was wrong with my fiction.

Needless to say, since I was writing fiction throughout this period, and since Lennis Dunlap has a mind worth consulting, from time to time I showed him my own fiction. He went over it with the same eye for detail he gave to our work on other people's writing, and though I cannot say he wasn't helpful, I soon learned the limits of even the best advice. Coming from Tennessee, he did not speak the same English I speak, or know the same kinds of people, or interpret life experience in quite the same ways I do. When he suggested changes and I accepted his suggestions, the story almost invariably went wrong. What I learned from him, in short, is that a writer must take infinite pains—if he writes only one great story in his life, that is better than writing a hundred bad ones—and that finally the pains the writer takes must be his own.

2

Another indicator of the young writer's talent is the relative accuracy and originality of his "eye." The good writer sees things sharply, vividly, accurately, and selectively (that is, he chooses what's important), not necessarily because his power of observation is by nature more acute than that of other people (though by practice it becomes so), but because he cares about seeing things clearly and getting them down effectively. Partly he cares because he knows that careless seeing can undermine his project. Imagining the fictional scene imprecisely—failing to notice, for instance, the gesture that would in real life accompany some assertion by a character (the dismissive wave that takes back part of what has been said, or the clenched fist that reveals stronger emotion than the character has expressed) —the writer may be tricked into developing his situation in some way that is unconvincing. This is perhaps the chief offense in bad fiction: we sense that characters are being manipulated, forced to do things they would not really do. The bad writer may not intend to manipulate; he simply does not know what his characters would do because he has not been watching them closely enough in his mind's eye—has not been catching the subtle emotional signals that, for the more careful writer, show where the action must go next. Both because the cogency of his story depends on it and because he has learned to take pride in getting his scenes exactly right, the good writer scrutinizes the imagined or remembered scene with full concentration. Though his plot seems to be rolling along beautifully and his characters seem to be behaving with authentic and surprising independence, as characters in good fiction always do, the writer is willing to stop writing for a minute or two, or even stop for a long while, to figure out precisely what some object or gesture looks like and hunt down exactly the right words to describe it.

One of the best eyes in recent fiction belongs to the novelist David Rhodes. Look closely at the following:

> The old people remember Della and Wilson Montgomery as
> clearly as if just last Sunday after the church pot-luck dinner they
> had climbed into their gray Chevrolet and driven back out to

their country home, Della waving from the window and Wilson leaning over the wheel, steering with both hands. They can remember as if just yesterday they had driven by the Montgomerys' brownstone house and seen them sitting on their porch swing, Wilson rocking it slowly and conscientiously back and forth, Della smiling, her small feet only touching the floor on the back swing, both of them looking like careful, quiet children.

Della's hands were so small they could be put into small-mouth jars. For many years she was their only schoolteacher, and, except for the younger ones, they all had her, and wanted desperately to do well with spelling and numbers to please her. Without fail, screaming children would hush and hum in her arms. It was thought, among the women, that it was not necessary to seek help or comfort in times of need, because Della would sense it in the air and come. The old people don't talk of her now but what a shadow is cast over their faces and they seem to be talking about parts of themselves—not just that Della belonged to the old days, but that when she and Wilson were gone it was unnatural that anything else from back then should go on without them.*

The first visual detail in this passage, the abstractly introduced pot-luck dinner, is not especially remarkable: anyone dealing with this culture might have thought of it, and Rhodes doesn't dwell on it, though it's worth including as a quick way of characterizing Della and Wilson Montgomery. The "gray Chevrolet" is a little more specific, with its useful connotations of drabness, humble normality; but it's with the next image that Rhodes begins to bear down: Della waving, Wilson "leaning over the wheel, steering with both hands." The image of Wilson, though not extraordinary, is specific and vivid; we recognize that we're dealing with a careful author, one worth our trust. We see more than that Wilson leans over the wheel and steers with both hands: we see, for some reason, the expression on his face, something about his age; we know, without asking ourselves how we know, that he's wearing a hat. (Hints of his

*David Rhodes, *Rock Island Line* (New York: Harper & Row, 1975), p. 1.

nearsightedness, nervousness, age, and culture lead us to un-conscious generalization.) In other words, by selecting the right detail, the writer subtly suggests others; the telling detail tells us more than it says.

Now the images become much sharper: on the porch swing, Wilson rocks slowly and *conscientiously*—a startling word that makes the scene spring to life (adverbs are either the dullest tools or the sharpest in the novelist's toolbox)—and then, better yet: "Della smiling, her small feet only touching the floor on the back swing, both of them looking like careful, quiet children." Only the keenest novelistic eye would notice where it is that the feet touch; only a fine novelistic mind would understand how much that detail tells us of how Della sits, how she feels; and yet Rhodes treats it as a passing detail, moving on to his climactic image, "like careful, quiet children."

The first line of the second paragraph, "Della's hands were so small they could be put into small-mouth jars," presents a new level of technique, as when a magician who's been doing rather ordinary tricks suddenly reveals how good he really is. It matters, of course, that the jars are a part of Della's country culture, but that's the least of it. No general statement, such as "Della had small hands," could touch the vividness of this image. We do not doubt, as we read, that any grown woman's hands could be so small (though it's questionable); we accept the metaphor and all it carries in its train—Della's childlike character and delicacy, her dutifulness and devotion (canning food), her saintly abstractedness, a quality hard to account for in terms of anything Rhodes has said, yet somehow present. After this, we are willing to accept quite odd assertions—that her pupils strain to please her, that children stop crying in her arms (they even "hush and hum"), and that intelligent, grown women somehow think they have no need to call her when they need her. And now, just when things are turning a touch mystical, Rhodes introduces another sharply observed detail:

when those who remember her talk of Della, "a shadow is cast over their faces and they seem to be talking about parts of themselves." The old people, in other words, think of Della Montgomery as they think of their own failing kidneys, slight chest pains, or arthritic fingers. What Rhodes' eye has caught is the queer similarity of people's expressions when they talk of their own lost youth and approaching death, on one hand, and, on the other, their feelings about the long-absent Della. Who wouldn't raptly turn the page and read on?

Rhodes' eye, like any fine novelist's, is accurate both about literal details (where one's feet touch on a porch swing) and about metaphorical equivalencies. Sitting in his study twenty years later, he summons in his mind's eye exactly how things looked and finds precise expression for what he sees, sometimes literal expression (Wilson bending over the steering wheel, Della's feet as she swings), sometimes metaphorical expression (the point that the two are like quiet, careful children, the point that the old people, talking about Della, wear the same look they wear when talking about parts of their own lives). The visual power of metaphor, it should be noticed, is as available to novelists as to poets. Often an important gesture or complex of gestures (the man who walks through a hostile crowd like a tired plowhorse, the man who jerks up and looks at his alarm clock like a startled chicken) cannot be captured so efficiently by any other means. Rhodes, like many good writers, depends at least as heavily on metaphor as on the naming of significant details. The main point to be noticed here, however, is that nothing in Rhodes' vision is secondhand: what he offers he has taken from life experience, not from Faulkner or, say, *Kojak*.

The unpromising writer sees derivatively. I once visited a class taught by a graduate-student creative writing teacher, one of whose methods was the use of psychodrama. While three students performed the psychodrama assigned, the rest of the class was to write a description of what each of them saw. The performers were asked to play the parts of a psychologist, a troubled mother, and a tuned-out, pot-smoking, troublesome son. The mother and son arrive, the mother explains her problem to the psychologist, and the son puts his feet on the psychologist's desk, defending his behavior at home only insofar as he's forced to do so. One of the most interesting things that happened in this psychodrama was that the woman playing psychologist, in trying to get the son to explain himself, repeatedly held out her hands to him, then looped them back like a seaman drawing in rope, saying in gesture, "Come on, come on! What have you to say?"—to which the son responded with sullen silence. When the drama was over and the descriptions by the class were read, not one student writer had caught the odd rope-pulling gesture. They caught the son's hostile feet on the desk, the mother's fumbling with her cigarettes, the son's repeated swipes of one hand through his already tousled hair —they caught everything they'd seen many times on TV, but not the rope gesture.

Much of the dialogue one encounters in student fiction, as well as plot, gesture, even setting, comes not from life but from life filtered through TV. Many student writers seem unable to tell their own most important stories—the death of a father, the first disillusionment in love—except in the molds and formulas of TV. One can spot the difference at once because TV is of necessity—given its commercial pressures—false to life. Films and series installments on TV are tremendously expensive, though less expensive than commercials. Costs change, always for the worse, but when I was last involved with TV work, a few years ago, a hundred thousand dollars a minute was not unusual. If you're putting together a thirteen-installment series for TV, you look for ways to beat the numbers. You set up your lights, cameras, and so on, at a particular location—Hollywood and Vine, or Lexington and Fifty-third—and you show the actors their tapes (the places where their feet must go), and you hand each of them a pink slip of paper with words on it, such as, "Walter? I haven't seen him. I swear it!" or, "Oh, Michael! Not again!" (Sometimes the lines have directions: *angrily*, or *wearily*, or *obviously lying*.) You shoot the scene, send the actors to the wardrobe truck for a change of clothes, then hand the actors a different set of slips (it may be a slightly different set of actors), and you shoot a second scene, which will be edited into a wholly different episode in the series. The point is that it pays to make the most of any given location and setup. In this kind of production nobody but the director— sometimes not even the director—knows what the story is. For this reason a serious, thoughtful speech is impossible in the ordinary television series. Any good actor can say, "Walter? I haven't seen him," with conviction; but if you hand him a difficult, thoughtful set of lines, the actor is likely to ask, "What's the context?" TV production costs often prohibit serious concern about context.

I am not denying that TV has value—as an opiate, if nothing else. My point is only that TV is not life, and the young novelist who has watched TV and failed to notice the difference is in trouble, except perhaps if his ultimate goal is to write for TV. (TV movies are sometimes more artistic. Interesting speeches are allowable, up to a point, since TV movie production allows more rehearsal and shooting time than does the usual TV series; but commercial pressures are never entirely absent. The beginning TV writer is given precise instructions on how to time his dramatic crescendos so that they lead to the breaks for "messages.")

What is wrong with the young writer who imitates TV instead of life is essentially no different from what's wrong with the young writer who imitates some earlier writer. It may feel more classy to imitate James Joyce or Walker Percy than *All in the Family*; but every literary imitation lacks something we expect of good writing: the writer seeing with his own eyes.

This is not to say that imitation cannot be a useful tool of the writer's apprenticeship. Some writing teachers favor literary imitation as a means of learning, and in the eighteenth century imitation was the chief way of learning to write. As I said earlier, one can learn a good deal by typing out, word for word, a great writer's story: the activity helps the beginning writer pay close attention. And one can learn by studying a writer one admires and transforming all he says to one's own way of seeing. But as a rule, the more closely one looks at the writer one admires, the more clearly one sees that his way can never be one's own. Open a novel of Faulkner's and copy a few paragraphs, but change the particulars to fit the world you know yourself. Take, for instance, the opening of Faulkner's *The Hamlet*:

> Frenchman's Bend was a section of rich river-bottom country lying twenty-miles southeast of Jefferson. Hill-cradled and remote, definite yet without boundaries, it had been the original grant site of . . .

If I were to translate this to something I know, I might begin:

> Putnam Settlement was a section of drab high ground in low, drab country, six miles south of Batavia. . . .

Already I find myself in trouble. People in western New York don't think in terms of "sections"; I must substitute some more appropriate word, and except for some vague evasion like "stretch," I can think of no word the people with whom I'm familiar would really use. Moreover, Putnam Settlement would not think of itself in relation to Batavia or anywhere else, partly because Putnam Settlement, like Batavia, isn't really a "place," not even a "definite yet without boundaries" sort of place. Faulkner has treated in his opening sentence something of grave importance to those who proudly proclaim themselves Southerners, namely, place and all that implies— history, kin connections, identity. Perhaps because they were never humiliated by the loss of a civil war, perhaps because their culture is more open to strangers, perhaps for other reasons, western New Yorkers don't feel the same fierce concern about place that traditional Southerners feel. Where I come from, one place runs into another without much noticing. Place names are less matters of pride than points of orientation. Not far from Putnam Settlement there's a village called Brookville where there hasn't been a house or barn in years. People still speak of it as if they knew what they meant, which they do, but no one knows who lived there in 1800 or would dream of describing it to a stranger as a place. One mentions Brookville when directing someone to Charley Walsh's farm.

Faulkner's second sentence, "Hill-cradled and remote . . . ," raises further problems. First there's the sonorous Southern grandeur of the opening phrase, with its rhetorical suspension of meaning. Anyone with Putnam Settlement in mind would be embarrassed to be caught framing sentences in the style of a congressman or the *National Geographic*. The place, insofar as it is one, won't support it. (That's why people frequently don't talk, in western New York; they just point.) Nor would anyone who lives in the proximity of Putnam Settlement think about mentioning the lay of the land. If you live in rich bottom country with hills surrounding, like the people of Faulkner's Frenchman's Bend, it makes sense to think in terms of large, enclosed landscapes. In Putnam Settlement you think of the weeds along the road (Queen Anne's lace), the large, dead cherry and apple trees, the sagging, long-since-abandoned barns. The main value of trying to use Faulknerian devices for western New York turns out to be that the attempt shows dramatically how subject matter influences style.

A good novelist creates powerfully vivid images in the reader's mind, and nothing is more natural than that the beginning novelist should try to imitate the effects of some master, because he loves that writer's vivid world. But finally imitation is a bad idea. What writers of the past saw and said, even the recent past, is history. It is obvious that no one any longer talks or thinks like the characters of Jane Austen or Charles Dickens. It is perhaps less obvious that hardly anyone under thirty talks like the characters of Saul Bellow or his imitators. The beginning novelist can learn from his betters their tricks of accurate observation, but what he sees must be his own time and place or else, as in the very best historical fiction, the past as we, with our special sensibility (not better but new), would see it if we went back. The beginning writer need not worry too much if his work is in trivial respects derivative—in fact, nothing is more tiresome than writing that strains after what the poet Anthony Hecht once called "a fraudulent and adventitious novelty." Aping another writer's style is foolish, but the noblest originality is not stylistic but visionary and intellectual; the writer's accurate presentation of what he, himself, has seen, heard, thought, and felt.

The writer's accuracy of eye has partly to do with his character. For some novelists, as for most poets and many short story writers, the main accuracy required by their art has to do with self-understanding. Novelists of this kind—Beckett, Proust, many writers who favor first-person narration—specialize in private vision. What they need to see clearly and document well is their own feelings, experience, prejudice. Such a novelist may hate nearly all of humanity, as Céline does, or large groups of people, as does Nabokov. What counts in this case is not that we believe the private vision to be right but that we are so convinced by and interested in the person who does the seeing that we are willing to follow him around. Sometimes, as in the case of a writer like Waugh, we laugh at a misanthropic cynicism we would not consider adopting for ourselves—much as we might laugh at an amusing crank at a party. All that is required to keep us following such a writer is that he fully understand that he is, in the ordinary view, a crackpot, and that he present himself as such, creating a distinct and interesting persona. He must work up his act with the skill of a master clown—however grim his ultimate purpose—understanding how normal people are likely to react to him and manipulating that reaction to his advantage. In other words, he must understand, with a full measure of ironic detachment, his tics and oddities, so that he can present them to us by conscious art, and not by slips that cause us embarrassment for him and lead us to avoid him. Think of the superbly controlled sadist-snob image Alfred Hitchcock created for himself. Think of Nabokov as he presented himself both in his writing and in television interviews; using a snob accent as artfully fabricated as the language of Donald Duck, he reveled in such goofiness as, breaking in on himself, "Careful now! Here comes a metaphor!" The persona need not be comic, as these examples would seem to suggest. Another writer might play Wolfman; yet another might put on, as William S. Burroughs has done, the zombie style.

If we ask ourselves what usefulness or value such writers have, we at once recognize that they're so various as to make no single answer possible. Some, like Evelyn Waugh, allow us the pleasure of a moral holiday: we relax our fair-mindedness and civility and for a brief period take nasty delight in hearing the worst said of people and institutions we, too, in our more childish moments, love to scorn. Some, like Nabokov, present serious and moral visions of the world but do it in such a way (by irony and nastiness) that no underlying softness or piety undermines the effect. Some, like Donald Barthelme, simply present themselves as fascinating oddities of nature—or of literature gone awry. The list of possibilities might be extended. What all such writers have in common is their bold idiosyncrasy, their happy pursuit of their own unique paths in the labyrinthine pluralistic woods. Sometimes such writers explicitly deny, as William Gass does, that fiction is capable of presenting anything broader than a quirky individual vision. Whatever their claims, they present, in effect, portraits or comic cartoons of the artist, and we judge them exactly as we judge stand-up comedians like Bill Cosby or comic actors like

W. C. Fields, by the consistency and accuracy of observation with which they present to us their staged selves, their friends, enemies, memories, peculiar hopes and crank opinions.

For another kind of novelist the accuracy required is, I think, of a higher order, infinitely more difficult to achieve. This is the novelist who moves like a daemon from one body —one character—to another. Rather than master the tics and oddities of his own being and learn how to present them in an appealing way—and rather than capture other people in the manner of a cunning epigrammist or malicious gossip—he must learn to step outside himself, see and feel things from every human—and inhuman—point of view. He must be able to report, with convincing precision, how the world looks to a child, a young woman, an elderly murderer, or the governor of Utah. He must learn, by staring intently into the dream he dreams over his typewriter, to distinguish the subtlest differences between the speech and feeling of his various characters, himself as impartial and detached as God, giving all human beings their due and acknowledging their frailties. Insofar as he pretends not to private vision but to omniscience, he cannot as a rule, love some of his characters and despise others.

What chiefly astonishes us in the work of this highest class of novelists—Tolstoy, Dostoevsky, Mann, Faulkner—is the writer's gift for rendering the precise observations and feelings of a wide variety of characters, even entering the minds (in Tolstoy's case) of animals. The beginning novelist who has the gift for inhabiting other lives has perhaps the best chance for success.

The writer who does not have this gift can usually develop it to some extent, once he has decided he needs it. True, if his irrational hatreds or loves run deep he may be permanently stymied. (No one readily admits that his hatreds are irrational. The stubborn conviction that one is right to spurn most kinds of people can itself be a stymieing force. Character defects fed by self-congratulation are the hardest to shed.) Once one has recognized that the novelist ought to be able to play advocate for all kinds of human beings, see through their eyes, feel with their nerves, accept their stupidest settled opinions as self-evident facts (for them), one simply begins to do it; and doing it again and again—carefully rereading, reconsidering, revising—one gets good at it.

By certain tricks and certain exercises one can sharpen one's gift for seeing the world as others see it. Every writer finds his own. Some may pore over fat astrology books, not for comfort or a head start on disaster but for hints to the complex oddities of human character (the total character of a Pisces vs. the total character of a Leo, whether or not one believes these respective traits have to do with people's birth dates). Some read psychological case studies or "ladies' magazines" or, alas, "men's"; some play with phrenology, palmistry, or the Tarot. What one has to get, one way or another, is insight—not just knowledge—into personalities not visibly like one's own. What one needs is not the facts but the "feel" of the person not oneself.

For some people, of course, no tricks or exercises can help. For one reason or another these people seem never able to guess what others are thinking and feeling. They walk through a lifelong mystery, wondering why people are smiling at them or frowning at them, puzzling over exactly what so-and-so might have meant by that kiss on the cheek or that peculiar sneer in the supermarket. What works for most human beings doesn't work for them. We see a given expression on someone's face, and by mentally or even physically imitating that expression we understand what *we* would have meant by it, and by a leap of faith we assume that the other person meant the same. Or someone speaks crossly to us for no apparent reason, and on the basis of the theory that other people are essentially like ourselves we are able to figure out the real or imagined slight, or the stomach pain, or whatever, that caused the person's anger. Why some people cannot do this (assuming that we who think we can are not fooling ourselves) is probably a question for psychologists. It seems obvious that at least in some cases the problem lies in a neurosis. We have all encountered people who displace their anger at parents or themselves into anger at some social group: the Klansman who hates liberals and imputes evil motives to the liberal's most casual remarks, or the liberal who confidently imputes racial bigotry to anyone who expresses doubt about the value of welfare programs. But whatever the cause, it seems likely that some people can never learn to empathize with their neighbors, at least not with the confidence and clarity it takes to be a novelist of Tolstoy's kind. Such people have no choice, if they wish to be novelists, but to be the spokesmen of private, idiosyncratic vision. They are committed by character to one kind of novel and not the other.

To be psychologically suited for membership in what I have called the highest class of novelists, the writer must be not only capable of understanding people different from himself but fascinated by such people. He must have sufficient self-esteem that he is not threatened by difference, and sufficient warmth and sympathy, and a sufficient concern with fairness, that he wants to value people different from himself, and finally he must have, I think, sufficient faith in the goodness of life that he can not only tolerate but celebrate a world of differences, conflicts, oppositions.

Both the novelist of idiosyncratic vision and the novelist who seeks a more dispassionate understanding can improve the vividness of his fiction by learning to see characters in the light of their metaphoric equivalencies, though in one case the character who emerges will be someone seen from outside, colored by the writer's bias, and in the other case the character may seem someone as real and complex as we are ourselves. Perhaps the best exercise for heightening one's gift for discovering such equivalencies is the game called "Smoke." The player who is

It thinks of some personage living or dead and gives his fellow players a starting clue—"living American," "dead Asian," or whatever—then each player in turn asks a question in the form: "What kind of ———— are you?" (What kind of smoke, what kind of vegetable, what kind of weather, building, part of the body, and so forth.) As the answers pile up, everyone playing the game finds he has a clearer and clearer sense of the personage whose name he is seeking, and when someone finally guesses the right answer, the effect is likely to have something like the power of a mystical revelation. No one who has played the game with even moderately competent players—people capable of suspending intellect for the deeper knowledge of the poetic mind—can doubt the value of metaphor for the creation of vivid character.

The writer with a truly accurate eye (and ear, nose, sense of touch, etc.) has an advantage over the writer who does not in that, among other things, he can tell his story in concrete terms, not just feeble abstractions. Instead of writing, "She felt terrible," he can show—by the precise gesture or look or by capturing the character's exact turn of phrase—subtle nuances of the character's feeling. The more abstract a piece of writing is, the less vivid the dream it sets off in the reader's mind. One can feel sad or happy or bored or cross in a thousand ways: the abstract adjective says almost nothing. The precise gesture nails down the one feeling right for the moment. This is what is meant when writing teachers say that one should "show," not "tell." And this, it should be added, is *all* that the writing teacher means. Good writers may "tell" about almost anything in fiction except the characters' feelings. One may tell the reader that the character went to a private school (one need not show a scene at the private school if the scene has no importance for the rest of the narrative), or one may tell the reader that the character hates spaghetti; but with rare exceptions the characters' feelings must be demonstrated: fear, love, excitement, doubt, embarrassment, despair become real only when they take the form of events—action (or gesture), dialogue, or physical reaction to setting. Detail is the lifeblood of fiction.

3

Another indicator of the novelist's talent is intelligence—a certain kind of intelligence, not the mathematician's or the philosopher's but the storyteller's—an intelligence no less subtle than the mathematician's or the philosopher's but not so easily recognized.

Like other kinds of intelligence, the storyteller's is partly natural, partly trained. It is composed of several qualities, most of which, in normal people, are signs of either immaturity or incivility: wit (a tendency to make irreverent connections); obstinacy and a tendency toward churlishness (a refusal to believe what all sensible people know is true); childishness (an apparent lack of mental focus and serious life purpose, a fondness for daydreaming and telling pointless lies, a lack of proper respect, mischievousness, an unseemly propensity for crying over nothing); a marked tendency toward oral or anal fixation or both (the oral manifested by excessive eating, drinking, smoking, and chattering; the anal by nervous cleanliness and neatness coupled with a weird fascination with dirty jokes); remarkable powers of eidetic recall, or visual memory (a usual feature of early adolescence and mental retardation); a strange admixture of shameless playfulness and embarrassing earnestness, the latter often heightened by irrationally intense feelings for or against religion; patience like a cat's; a criminal streak of cunning; psychological instability; recklessness, impulsiveness, and improvidence; and finally, an inexplicable and incurable addiction to stories, written or oral, bad or good. Not all writers have exactly these same virtues, of course. Occasionally one finds one who is not abnormally improvident.

I have described here, you may think, a curious and dangerous beast. (In fact, good writers are almost never dangerous—a point I will need to develop, but not just yet.) Though the tone is half-joking, my description of the writer is meant to be accurate. Writers would clearly be madmen if they weren't so psychologically complicated ("too complex," a famous psychiatrist once wrote, "to settle on any given madness")—and some go mad anyway. The easiest way to talk about this special sort of intelligence is perhaps to describe what it does, what the young novelist must sooner or later be equipped to do.

I have said that writers are addicted to stories, written or oral, bad or good. I do not mean, of course, that they can't tell the difference between bad and good stories, and I must now add that some bad stories make them furious. (Some writers get more angry, some less; some, in the presence of the kind of fiction that makes other good writers howl and throw things, do not show their anger, but turn their fury inward, sinking into suicidal gloom.) The kind of fiction that makes good writers cross is not *really* bad fiction. Most writers will occasionally glance through a comic book or a western, even a nurse novel if they find it at the doctor's office, and finish the thing with no hard feelings. Some happily read bad and good detective fiction, sci-fi's, sodbusters (fat novels about families in the South or West), even—perhaps especially—children's books. What makes them angry is bad "good" fiction, whether it's for children or for grownups.

It would be a mistake to blame the anger on professional jealousy. No one is more generous with his praise than a novelist who has just read a good novel by someone else, even if the author has been his lifelong enemy. One may be nearer the mark in blaming the anger on the novelist's insecurity, though that is not quite right, either. If one works very hard at doing a thing one considers important (telling a story extremely well), one is annoyed to see someone else do it badly or, worse, fraudulently, while claiming to belong in the same high league. One's honor is sullied—the honor of the whole profession is sullied—and one's purpose in life is undermined, especially if readers and reviewers seem unable to tell the difference between the real thing and the fake, as often they can't. One begins to doubt that one's standards have any value, even any roots in reality. One becomes crabby, petulant, eager to fight. Since excellence in the arts is a matter of taste—since one cannot really prove one work better than another, at least not in the same clear way mathematicians can prove one another right or wrong—the widespread celebration of a stupid book offends the true writer. Like a child who knows he's right but cannot make his parents see, and has neither the power nor the authority to beat them, the writer offended by an alleged masterpiece that he knows to be phony may throw the tantrums of the helpless, or sulk, or turn sly (may turn to, as Joyce put it, silence, exile, cunning).

Nothing is harder on the true writer's sense of security than an age of bad criticism, and in one way or another, sad to say, almost every age qualifies. No depressed and angry writer at the present moment can fail to notice, if he raises his heavy head and looks around, that fools, maniacs, and jabberers are everywhere—mindless, tasteless, ignorant schools of criticism publishing fat journals and meeting in solemn conclave, completely misreading great writers, or celebrating tawdry imitation writers to whom not even a common farm duck would give his ear; other schools maintaining, with much talk of Heidegger, that nothing a writer writes means anything, the very existence of his page is an amusing accident, all the words are a lunatic blithering (for all the writer's care), since language is by nature false and misleading, best read from the bottom of the page to the top. (Even Dante's *Divine Comedy*, critics like Harold Bloom and Stanley Fish maintain in their dissimilar ways, is mere raw material for "the art of criticism.") In a literary culture where the very notion of a "masterpiece" is commonly thought barbaric, where good writing is called reactionary or otherwise self-limiting, and where the worst writers are regularly admired (so it seems to the novelist in his gloomy funk, and a twenty-year list of best-sellers and Book-of-the-Month Club selections would prove him right), who's to say that all the carefully achieved standards of the bravest, most disciplined writer are not quackery and lob law? (Even in his funk the writer clings to his rhetoric and his OED.)

But it is not finally insecurity (his sense that his honor and purpose cannot survive the blind stampede of Nietzsche's "herd") that makes the true novelist hate fake art, though insecurity is involved. The practice of reading and writing fiction, like the practice of law or medicine, gives benefits only the man engaged in the practice can really know, know immediately and fully, in the quality of his life and vision. An analogy from the experience of painters may help. A man who regularly does oil paintings—landscapes, let us say—develops an acute eye for color and light, shapes, volumes, details of form. The novelist develops an acute eye, sometimes bordering on the psychic, for human feelings and behavior, tastes and habitats, pleasures, sufferings. The fake novelist not only fails to develop that gift but by his fakery impedes it, not only in himself but in his readers as well, at least insofar as they're tricked.

I said earlier that the writer who works closely with detail —studying his characters' most trivial gestures in the imagined scene to discover exactly where the scene must go next—is the writer most likely to persuade and awe us. That close scrutiny is one among many elements that make up the practice of fiction; let it serve as a clue to the value of authentic practice —and to the waste and harm in fictional malpractice. The true writer's scrutiny of imagined scenes both feeds on and feeds his real-life experience: almost without knowing he's doing it, the writer becomes an alert observer. He may even become such a watcher of people that he seems an oddity to his friends. It is said (I think—sometimes by accident I make these things up) that Anthony Trollope, when he went to a party, would sit for ten minutes or more, intently staring at one guest after another, hardly answering when people addressed him, much to the embarrassment of the company. Whether or not that story is true, it is a fact that a party with good writers can be, for the uninitiated, unnerving. Joyce Carol Oates's gazelle eyes dominate the room, especially when she chooses not to talk, trying to be (one suspects) inconspicuous. Stanley Elkin's style is to keep the floor at any cost, telling funny stories; but behind the thick glasses, the enlarged, keenly focused myopia makes the listener wonder if perhaps *he* will be the next funny story. (In fact, Elkin's stories are always generous. If anyone must play the fool in one, he takes the part for himself.) Bernard Malamud has an alarming way of listening when people speak. He focuses intently on gestures, turns of phrase; he may abruptly ask why the person speaking with him wears dark glasses. One could say the same kinds of things about other writers, though of course not about all other writers; many are highly socialized and never let it show that they are watching. The point is, whether or not they show it at dinner parties, writers learn, by a necessity of their trade, to be the sharpest of observers. That is one of the joys, as well as one of the curses, of the writer's occupation. Psychologists perhaps get some of this same pleasure, but psychologists, whatever their claims and intentions, are essentially interested in the aberrant mind. Writers care about all possibilities of human nature.

I might mention another embarrassment involved in the writer's habit of close attention. Once when I was driving through Colorado with a friend, traveling down a narrow mountain pass, we came upon an accident. A pickup truck and a car had collided, and from fifty feet away we could see the blood. We pulled over and ran to help. All the time I was running, all the time I was trying, with my friend's help, to pry open the door of the car in which a nine-months-pregnant woman had been impaled through the abdomen, I was thinking: I must remember this! I must remember my feelings! How would I describe this? I do not think I behaved less efficiently than my nonliterary friend, who was probably not thinking such thoughts; in fact, I may possibly have behaved more swiftly and efficiently, trying in my mind to create a noble scene. Nonetheless, what I felt above all was disgust at my mind's detachment, its inhumane fascination with the precise way the blood pumped, the way flesh around a wound becomes instantly proud, that is, puffed up, and so on. I would have been glad at that moment to be a literary innocent.

For better or worse, the practice of fiction changes a person. The true novelist knows things another man with his own specialization does not know and might not wish to. The false practitioner, on the other hand, knows less than nothing. Not only can it be said that reality is obscure to him; his bad techniques—his learned misapprehensions (think of the dis-Pollyanna science fiction writer)—distort his vision, so that he sees falsely. The true novelist despises the false one both because the false practitioner fools himself, manipulating characters instead of trying to understand them, and because he teaches his readers (at best) nothing.

What the novelist does besides despise false novels is try to write true ones. His complex intelligence, in other words, gathers its various and disparate powers to make up a satisfying story. The best way I can think of to make this point concrete is to speak of what good fiction requires.

Good fiction sets off, as I said earlier, a vivid and continuous dream in the reader's mind. It is "generous" in the sense that it is complete and self-contained: it answers, either explicitly or by implication, every reasonable question the reader can ask. It does not leave us hanging, unless the narrative itself justifies its inconclusiveness. It does not play pointlessly subtle games in which storytelling is confused with puzzle-making. It does not "test" the reader by demanding that he bring with him some special knowledge without which the events make no sense. In short, it seeks, without pandering, to satisfy and please. It is intellectually and emotionally significant. It is elegant and efficient; that is, it does not use more scenes, characters, physical details, and technical devices than it needs to do its job. It has design. It gives that special pleasure we get from watching, with appreciative and impressed eyes, a *performance*. In other words, noticing what it is that the writer has brought off, we feel well served: "How easy he makes it look!" we say, conscious of difficulties splendidly overcome. And finally, an aesthetically successful story will contain a sense of life's strangeness, however humdrum its makings.

If a young novelist fully appreciates all these qualities of successful fiction and regularly pursues them in his own work, one does not need to make guesses about his potential: he's already there. Most young novelists are aware of, and interested in, only some few of these qualities and might even deny that others are important. Partly this is an effect of lost innocence, the innocence the writer must now regain. Every child knows intuitively (insofar as he likes stories at all; some children don't) what the requirements are for good fiction, but by the time he's reached high-school age, he's grown a trifle confused, bullied by his teachers into reading what is in fact trash, scorned if he reads a good comic book, and warned, if he picks up *Crime and Punishment*, "Harold, you're not ready for that." By the time he's a sophomore or junior in college, he's likely to be quite profoundly confused, imagining, for instance, that "theme" is the most important value in fiction.

Nothing, let me pause to argue, could be farther from the truth than the notion that theme is all. Theme is what, at its deepest level, the story is about; it is the philosophical and emotional principle by which the writer selects and organizes his materials. Real literary artists are always conscious of their theme; but this does not assure good writing. Both theme and message (that is, subject and specific preachment) are likely to be more visible in a cheap western than in Proust's *Remem-*

brance of Things Past. And on the other hand, in some of our most beloved fictions the theme is difficult to isolate. What, exactly, is the theme of "Jack and the Beanstalk"? Any given reader may think he knows, but he should be given pause by the fact that for Bruno Bettelheim, whom most people would consider a competent psychologist (or at least not stupid), the story is about penis envy—surely a minority opinion. Some might say that the story is about the victory of childish innocence; some might say other things. The point is that what makes us take pleasure in "Jack and the Beanstalk" is not necessarily our sense, as we read or listen, that some basic philosophical question is being dramatized and illuminated, though in other fictions theme may indeed be what chiefly moves us. In *Pilgrim's Progress* the allegory may be the central appeal, though some might argue more or less persuasively that what we like most about that book is its style. Certainly, in Melville's *Bartleby the Scrivener* or Mann's *Death in Venice*, philosophical content is part of what holds us rapt. If theme is not what we chiefly love about a given story, not chiefly what makes us reread it and recommend it to our friends, then theme is not universally the most important quality of good fiction. Theme is like the floors and structural supports in a fine old mansion, indispensable but not, as a general rule, what takes the reader's breath away. More often than not, theme, or meaning, is the statement the architecture and decor make about the inhabitants. When we think about it, it seems to me, the all but universal fascination with theme in high-school and college English courses has to do with the teacher's need to say something intellectual and surprising. A flawlessly told story by Boccaccio, Balzac, or Borges is hard to talk about simply as a story, and since all stories "mean" things—sometimes quite odd and surprising things—the temptation to talk about the meaning rather than the story may be nearly irresistible.

For this reason the college-age student is easily persuaded to the view that great writers are primarily philosophers and teachers; they write to "show" us things. This is the message teachers and professional critics suggest in such misleading locutions as "Jean Rhys is *showing* us" or "Flaubert is *demonstrating* . . ." Teaching creative writing, one constantly hears students say of their work, "I am trying to show . . ." The error in this is obvious once it's pointed out. Does the twenty- or twenty-five-year-old writer really have brilliant insights that the intelligent reading public (doctors, lawyers, professors, skilled machinists, businessmen) has never before heard or thought of? If the young novelist's answer is an emphatic *yes*, he would do the world a favor by entering the ministry or the Communist party. If I belabor the point, I do so only because the effect of English literature courses is so often, for a certain kind of student, insidious.

Though it may not be universal, and though in any case it's a matter of degree, it often seems that people in their late teens or twenties cannot help but feel that their parents and most other so-called adults are fools, sell-outs, or at the very least, disappointing. Their disdain has partly to do with the developing psyche's struggle, the imperative Joyce treated, that the young animal assert his power and replace the elder. No doubt it is often a class trait: the child of the lower or lower middle class is urged in both overt and subtle ways to surpass his background, his well-meaning parents and friends never anticipating that if their dream of upward mobility is realized, the child may adopt the prejudices of the class to which he's lifted and, with a touch of neurotic distress, may permanently scorn his former life and also, to a certain extent, himself, since the class he's invaded is unlikely to accept him fully. And no doubt the arrogance of the young has also to do with the age-old idealism of teachers, who forever harp, not without some justice, on how the former generation failed and the world's salvation is up to the new generation. Whatever the cause, the young person—the young novelist—is encouraged to feel that *he* is life's hope, *he* is the Messiah.

There's nothing wrong with that feeling. It's natural—part of nature—and no artist ever became great by violating his deepest feelings, however youthful, neurotic, or wrongheaded. Nonetheless, adolescent emotion cannot create real art, usually, and if the young novelist can understand his inclination he can avoid an undue misuse of his energies. One of the great temptations of young writers is to believe that all the people in the subdivision in which he grew up were fools and hypocrites in need of blasting or instruction. As he matures, the writer will come to realize, with luck, that the people he scorned had important virtues, that they had better heads and hearts than he knew. The desire to show people proper beliefs and attitudes is inimical to the noblest impulses of fiction.

In the final analysis, what counts is not the philosophy of the writer (that will reveal itself in any case) but the fortunes of the characters, how their principles of generosity or stubborn honesty or stinginess or cowardice help them or hurt them in specific situations. What counts is the characters' story.

Just as it is easy for the student of literature to believe he, his teacher, and his classmates are better people than those unfamiliar with Ezra Pound, it is easy for him to be persuaded by his coursework that "entertainment" is a low if not despicable value in literature. Properly indoctrinated, the student may come to be convinced that certain classics he instinctively dismissed, at first, as insipid (good candidates, some would say, are Langland's *Piers Plowman* and Richardson's *Clarissa*) are in fact immensely interesting books, though not entertaining in the common sense, like the *Canterbury Tales*, or *Tom Jones*, or the sci-fi of Walter M. Miller, Jr. (*A Canticle for Leibowitz*). If he takes enough English literature courses, the young would-be writer can learn to block every true instinct he has. He learns to dismiss from mind the persistent mean streak in J. D. Salinger, the tough-guy whining sentimentality in Hemingway, Faulkner's bad habit of breaking the vivid and continuous dream by pouring on the rhetoric, Joyce's mannerisms, Nabokov's frigidity. He can learn that writers he at first thought quite good, usually women (Margaret Mitchell, Pearl Buck, Edith Wharton, Jean Rhys), are "really" second class. With the right teacher he can learn that Homer's *Iliad* is a poem against war, that the *Canterbury Tales* is a disguised sermon, or—if he studies with Professor Stanley Fish and his cohorts—that we have no objective grounds for saying that Shakespeare's work is "better" than that of Mickey Spillane. If he also takes courses in creative writing, he may learn that one should always write about what one knows, that the most important thing in fiction is point of view, perhaps even that plot and character are the marks of antiquated fiction. To a wise and secure innocent all this would seem very odd, but students in a college classroom are defenseless, and the rewards offered for giving in are many, the chief one being the seductive sweetness of literary elitism.

It is the power of miseducation's blandishments that makes stubbornness, even churlishness, a valuable quality in young writers. The good young writer, the potentially successful one, knows what he knows and will not budge—chiefly knows that the first quality of good storytelling is storytelling. A profound theme is of trifling importance if the characters knocked around by it are uninteresting, and brilliant technique is a nuisance if it pointlessly prevents us from seeing the characters and what they do.

The stubbornness that saves a writer in college will continue to serve him all his life, guarding and preserving his ego if the world refuses to notice how good he is and saving him, if necessary, from the potential suckerdom of fame. (The famous author tends to be less meticulously edited than the unknown one, tends to be asked for his opinion on subjects he knows nothing about, tends to be sought out for reviews or jacket blurbs of bad books by his friends.) And stubbornness will prove useful, in later life as in college, in protecting the writer from those who try to give him bad advice. As inept college writing teachers try to get the beginning writer to write fiction more like that of Jane Austen, or Grace Paley, or Raymond Carver, so well-meaning nincompoops later (editors, reviewers, academicians) are sure to put pressure on the writer to make him more nearly what they would be if they could write fiction. Not, of course, that the writer's stubbornness should be absolute. Some advice turns out to be good, however distasteful at first.

If the writer understands that stories are first and foremost stories, and that the best stories set off a vivid and continuous dream, he can hardly help becoming interested in technique, since it is mainly bad technique that breaks the continuousness and checks the growth of the fictional dream. He quickly discovers that when he unfairly manipulates his fiction—pushing the characters around by making them do things they wouldn't do if they were free of him; or laying on the symbolism (so that the strength of the fiction is diminished, too much of its energy going into mere intellect); or breaking in on the action to preach (however important the truth he's out to preach); or pumping up his style so that it becomes more visible than even the most interesting of his characters—the writer, by these clumsy moves, impairs his fiction. To notice such faults is to begin to correct them. One reads other writers to see how they do it (how they avoid overt manipulation), or one reads books about writing—even the worst are likely to be of some use—and above all, one writes and writes and writes. Let me add, before I leave this subject, that when he reads the work of other writers, the young novelist should read not in the manner of an English major but in the manner of a novelist. The good English major studies a work to understand and appreciate its meaning, to perceive its relationship to other works of the period, and so on. The young writer should read to see how effects are achieved, how things are done, sometimes reflecting on what he would have done in the same situation and on whether his way would have been better or worse, and why. He reads the way a young architect looks at a building, or a medical student watches an operation, both devotedly, hoping to learn from a master, and critically, alert for any possible mistake.

The development of fully competent technique calls for further psychological armor. If a writer learns his craft slowly and carefully, laboriously strengthening his style, not publishing too fast, people may begin to look at the writer aslant and ask suspiciously, "And what do *you* do?" meaning: "How come you sit around all the time? How come your dog's so thin?" Here the virtue of childishness is helpful—the writer's refusal to be serious about life, his mischievousness, and his tendency to cry, especially when drunk, a trick that makes persecutors quit. If the pressure grows intense, the oral and anal fixations swing into action: one relieves pressure by chewing things, chattering mindlessly, or straightening and re-straightening one's clothes.

The point is a serious one, and I do not mean to trivialize it. In my own experience, nothing is harder for the developing writer than overcoming his anxiety that he is fooling himself and cheating or embarrassing his family and friends. To most people, even those who don't read much, there is something special and vaguely magical about writing, and it is not easy for them to believe that someone they know—someone quite ordinary in many respects—can really do it. They tend to feel for the young writer a mixture of fond admiration and pity, a sense that the poor fellow is somehow maladjusted or misinformed. No human activity I know of takes more time than writing: it's highly unusual for anyone to become a successful writer if he cannot put in several hours every day at his typewriter. (Even for a successful professional, it can take a while to get into the mood, takes hours to get a few good pages of rough draft, and many many hours to revise them until they will bear repeated readings.) Of necessity the writer is unlike those of his friends who quit work at five; if he has a wife and children, the writer cannot pay as much attention to them as his neighbors do to theirs, and if the writer is worthy of his profession, he feels some guilt over this. Because his art is such a difficult one, the writer is not likely to advance in the world as visibly as do his neighbors: while his best friends from high school or college are becoming junior partners in prestigious law firms, or opening their own mortuaries, the writer may be still sweating out his first novel. Even if he has published a story or two in respectable periodicals, the writer doubts himself. In my teaching years, I have again and again seen young writers with obvious talent berate themselves almost to the point of paralysis because they feel they're not fulfilling their family and social obligations, feel—even when several stories have been accepted—that they're deluding themselves. Each rejection letter is shattering, and a parent's gentle prod— "Don't you think it's time you had children, Martha?"—can be an occasion of spiritual crisis. Only strong character, reinforced by the encouragement of a few people who believe in the writer, can get one through this period. The writer must somehow convince himself that he *is* in fact serious about life, so serious that he is willing to take great risks. He must find ways—mischievous humor, or whatever—of deflecting malicious or benevolent blows to his ego.

Only the writer who has come to understand how difficult it is simply to tell a first-rate story—with no cheap manipulations, no breaks in the dream, no preening or self-consciousness—is able to appreciate fully the quality of "generosity" in fiction. In the best fiction, plot is not a series of surprises but an increasingly moving series of recognitions, or moments of understanding. One of the most common mistakes among young writers (those who understand that fiction is storytelling) is the idea that a story gets its power from withheld information—that is, from the writer's setting the reader up and then bushwhacking him. Ungenerous fiction is first and foremost fiction in which the writer is unwilling to take the reader as an equal partner.

Say, for example, that the writer has decided to tell the story of a man who has moved into the house next door to the house of his teen-age daughter, a girl who does not know that the man is her father. The man—call him Frank—does not tell the girl—she may as well be Wanda—that she is his daughter. They become friends and, despite the difference in age, she begins to feel a sexual attraction.

What the foolish or inexperienced writer does with this idea is hide the father-daughter relationship from the reader as well as from the daughter until the last minute, at which point he jumps out and yells: "Surprise!" If the writer tells the story from the father's point of view and withholds the important information, the writer is false to the traditional reader-writer contract—that is, he has played a trick on the reader. (The so-called unreliable narrator favored in much contemporary fiction is not a violation of the contract. It is not the storyteller but a fictitious narrator, a character, that we must watch and learn to distrust. If the storyteller *himself* is unreliable, we avoid him as we would a mad sea captain or axe murderer.)

If, on the other hand, the story is told from the daughter's point of view, the device is legitimate, since the reader can only know what the daughter knows; but the writer has mishandled his idea. The daughter is simply a victim in this story, since she doesn't know the facts by means of which she could make significant choices—namely, struggle with her feelings and come to some decision, accepting her role as daughter or else, conceivably, choosing to violate the incest taboo. When the central character is a victim, not someone who *does* but someone who's *done to*, there can be no real suspense. Admittedly it is not always easy to see, in great fiction, the central character's agency. The governess in James's *The Turn of the Screw* would hotly deny that she herself is acting in complicity with the forces of evil, but gradually, to our horror, we realize that she is; and some stories—for instance those of Kafka—adapt to the purposes of "serious" fiction the central device of a certain kind of comic fiction, the clown-hero knocked around by the universe, a character we laugh at because his misapplied strategies and beliefs parody our own. (It is not that Kafka's heroes —or Beckett's—do not try to do things; it is only that the things they try don't work.) In the final analysis, real suspense comes with moral dilemma and the courage to make and act upon choices. False suspense comes from the accidental and meaningless occurrence of one damned thing after another.

The wiser or more experienced writer gives the reader the information he needs to understand the story moment by moment, with the result that instead of asking, as he reads, "What's going to happen to the characters next?" the reader asks, "What will Frank do next? What would Wanda say if Frank were to . . ." and so on. Involving himself in the story in this way, the reader feels true suspense, which is to say, true concern for the characters. He takes an active part, however secondary, in the story's growth and development: he speculates, anticipates; and because he has been provided with relevant information, he is in a position to catch the mistake if the writer draws false or unconvincing conclusions, forcing the action in a direction it would not naturally go, or making the characters feel things no human being would really feel in the situation.

If Frank is clearly drawn and interesting, a lifelike human being, the reader worries about him, understands him, cares about the choices he makes. Thus if Frank at some point, out of cowardice or indecisiveness, makes a choice any decent human being would recognize as wrong, the reader will feel vicarious embarrassment and shame, as he would feel if some loved one, or the reader himself, were to make such a choice. If Frank sooner or later acts bravely, or at least honestly, selflessly, the reader will feel a thrill of pride as if he himself or some loved one had behaved well—a pride that, ultimately, expresses pleasure in what is best not just in the made-up character but in all humankind. If Frank finally behaves well, and Wanda shows unexpected (but not arbitrary or writer-manipulated) nobility, the reader will feel even better. This is the morality of fiction. The morality of the story of Frank and Wanda does not reside in their choosing not to commit incest or in their deciding they *will* commit incest. Good fiction does not deal in codes of conduct—at least not directly; it affirms responsible humanness.

The young writer who understands why it is wisest to tell the Frank and Wanda story as one of dilemma, suffering, and choice is in a position to understand good fiction's generosity in the broadest sense of the word. The wise writer counts on the characters and plot for his story's power, not on tricks of withheld information, including withheld information at the end—will they commit incest or won't they, now that they know? In other words, the writer lays himself wide open, dancing on a high wire without a net. The writer is generous, too, in that, for all his mastery of technique, he introduces only those techniques useful to the story: he is the story's servant, not a donzel for whom the story serves as an excuse to show off pyrotechnics. This is not to say that he's indifferent to the value of performance. Those techniques he uses because the story needs them he uses brilliantly. He works entirely in service of the story, but he works with class. On this, more later.

It is the importance of this quality of generosity in fiction that requires a measure of childishness in the writer. People who have strong mental focus and a sense of purpose in their lives, people who have respect for all that grownups generally respect (earning a good living, the flag, the school system, those who are richer than oneself, those who are beloved and famous, such as movie stars), are unlikely ever to make it through the many revisions it takes to tell a story beautifully, without visible tricks, nor would they be able to tolerate the fame and fortune of those who tell stories stupidly, with hundreds of tricks, all of them old and boring to the discriminating mind. First, with his stubborn churlishness the good writer scoffs at what the grownups are praising, then, with his childish forgetfulness and indifference to what sensible people think, he goes back to his foolish pastime, the making of real art.

The remaining qualities in good fiction, and the personality traits in the writer that are likely to help him achieve them, need not delay us long. Good fiction, I have said, is intellectually and emotionally significant. All this means is that a story with a stupid central idea, no matter how brilliantly the story is told, will be a stupid story. Take an easy example. A young newspaperman discovers that his father, who is the mayor of the city and has always been a hero to him, is the secret owner of brothels, sex shops, and a vicious loan-shark operation. Shall the newspaperman spill the beans on his father? Whatever his secret life, our newspaperman's father taught our newspaperman all the values he knows, including integrity, courage, and concern for the community. What is the newspaperman to do?

Who cares? The whole story is a moronic setup, good enough for writers of pop fiction but useless as a vehicle for art. The first thing wrong with it is that the clash of ideas implied is a clash of boring ideas, namely, which is more important, personal integrity (telling it like it is) or personal loyalty? Only very odd people don't realize that truth-telling is always a relative value. If you're living in Germany during World War II and a Jew is hiding in your basement, you do nothing wrong in the sight of God by telling the Nazi at the door you're the only one home. Personal integrity (not telling lies) is so obviously bendable in the name of a higher integrity that the question's not worth talking about. And in the case of this hypothetical story, the father's nastiness is so deep and broad (at least as we've set it up) that only a fool would agonize over the claim of personal loyalty. Almost no one doubts that personal loyalty is a good thing, up to a point: the worth of the value is transparent and needs no defense. It will be objected that the fictional situation I've just set up is almost exactly the situation in Robert Penn Warren's *All the King's Men*. I am tempted to answer, yes, that's so, and notice the streak of sentimentality that impairs that novel, from its tour-de-force opening blast of rhetoric through all its gothic delays to its end; but in fairness to the success of that book, despite its sentimentality, I must say, anticipating the next point I mean to turn to, it is Penn Warren's characters that save what might have been, in another writer's hands, a bad idea for a novel. If the essential plot idea is melodramatic, the complexity of the characters enriches and complicates the idea and partly saves it.

What is most deeply wrong with our newspaperman story idea is that it starts in the wrong place, not with character but with situation. Character is the very life of fiction. Setting exists so that the character has someplace to stand, something that can help define him, something he can pick up and throw, if necessary, or eat, or give to his girlfriend. Plot exists so the character can discover for himself (and in the process reveal to the reader) what he, the character, is really like: plot forces the character to choice and action, transforms him from a static construct to a lifelike human being making choices and paying for them or reaping the rewards. And theme exists only to make the character stand up and *be* somebody: theme is elevated critical language for what the character's main problem is.

Consider again our story of Frank and his daughter Wanda. One might write that story very well without ever bothering to figure out what the theme is: it would be enough for the writer to understand clearly that Frank has an interesting problem (some details of which the writer will have to pause and figure out). For some reason (any persuasive reason will do), Frank has moved next door to his daughter; he knows her, she doesn't know him (any explanation of this odd fact will suffice, as long as it's so convincing that no reader would think of doubting it); and he decides not to tell her (by reason of something in his character and situation; again, any reason will do, so long as it's convincing and fits with everything else in the story). Our character's interesting situation, then, is that *(a)* perhaps somewhat to his surprise, he begins to feel a father's love for, and maybe pride in, the daughter he never knew, and *(b)* he likes seeing her, the oftener the better, but *(c)* she's beginning to feel an undaughterly love for him, so that he must either tell her how things are or not tell her, and in either case the ultimate question is, What are they going to do?

Every detail that enters the story will have an influence on the degree to which the characters suffer and eventually on what they choose. Say the daughter lives with her stepfather and her mother is dead. If the stepfather is indifferent to her, or a drunkard, or crazy, or always away on trips to Cleveland, her admiration of Frank and her opportunity for seeing him will increase. Say Frank lost his daughter and now-dead wife because he spent seventeen years in prison, a fact of which he is bitterly ashamed. In this case both his longing for his daughter and his fear of telling her the truth may be intense. Obviously it doesn't matter which particulars the writer selects— if he's smart he'll simply select those details he'd most enjoy finding in a story by someone else—but whichever details he chooses, he commits himself to exploring those details for all significant implications.

The Frank-Wanda story, as we've begun to flesh it out, may at first glance seem as much a situation story as the newspaperman-and-his-father story, but on closer inspection we see it's not. The initial situation in the Frank-Wanda story exists because of a conflict within Frank's character: he simultaneously wants to reveal his identity to his daughter and also hide that identity, or to put the problem in broader philosophical terms, he wants to be both independent and involved—an impossibility. The internal conflict inevitably leads to an external conflict, easily dramatized: Wanda, falling in love with the man she doesn't know to be her father, must necessarily send out signals of her sexual interest and must necessarily receive confusing signals in return. We can predict the line of action: from joys to trouble and distress to spats and tears to revelation and decision. (There is nothing wrong with fiction in which the plot is relatively predictable. What matters is how things happen, and what it means that they happen, to the people directly involved and to the larger humanity for whom the characters serve as representatives. Needless to say, it is always best if the predictable comes in some surprising way.)

In nearly all good fiction, the basic—all but inescapable— plot form is: *A central character wants something, goes after it despite opposition (perhaps including his own doubts), and so arrives at a win, lose, or draw.* In a novel the pros and cons of the character's project get complicated (each force, pro or con, dramatized by minor characters, subplots, and so on), but the form, however disguised, remains. The "victim story," as I described it earlier, can never work because the victim cannot know and, out of that knowledge, act. (If the victim's desire is not to be a victim, and if he or she acts on it, the victim's story is not a "victim story.") I have said "nearly all good fiction," since we do find exceptions. I have already mentioned Kafka's use, and Beckett's, of the always unsuccessful clown-hero, and I should register in passing the special case of the "epiphany" story as Joyce developed it in *Dubliners*—a story form in which, for all practical purposes, the reader takes the place of the conventional central character: it is the reader who actively pursues, the reader who, at the climax of the story, achieves his "win"—a sudden shift of vision, a new understanding, an "epiphany." Not all of the stories in *Dubliners* work this way, of course; for example, "The Dead" does not. In any case, no one denies the effectiveness of epiphany fiction; but if my analysis of how it works is correct, it is closer to convention than it appears at first blush.

Before we leave our newspaperman story we should admit, reminded by Kafka's practice, that it does have one chance of success. All aesthetic rules give way for comedy. Let us say our newspaperman is a true dolt—but an interesting one. He believes fervently everything his father has ever said; his father's words are the law of his life. He also fervently loves his father. Obviously we are involved not in drama but in clown drama, the drama of lovable moron heroes like the Marx Brothers or Laurel and Hardy. The newspaperman (Laurel), his father (Hardy), and everybody else who blunders into the story must be, in effect, clowns whose comment on the human condition is not that of realistic fiction or even of, say, the gothic tale, with its systematically altered realism, but something quite different, a special kind of loving satire. The story can now work, at least theoretically, because, though the clash of ideas is not in itself interesting, the characters involved may be interesting and appealing, in a cartoonish way, and they're stupid enough to be interested in what we see through at once. Though the characters are patently inferior to us, their agonies, perplexities, and triumphs clowningly parallel our own. No one will claim that the story has been made intellectually significant, but it is at least no longer an expression of authorial weak-mindedness. As for the emotional significance of the piece, the only way we can judge such things, in the case of comedy, is by giving the story to readers and seeing if they laugh.

If the young writer is to achieve intellectual and emotional significance in his fiction, he must have the common sense to tell foolish ideas from interesting ones and important emotions from trivial ones. These abilities can be guided a little, for instance by the teacher's pointing out, as I've done above, that stories beginning in character and conflict are bound to be more interesting than stories that do not—a principle applicable even to thrillers, sodbusters, and horror stories. And the writer's sense of what questions are really interesting and what ones aren't worth bothering with may be heightened a little by wide reading, by conversation with intelligent people, and by the conscious attempt to, as James said, "be someone on whom nothing is lost."

On the whole, the capacity for recognizing the significant is a gift. It helps not to be a dupe, to be, instead, a person of independent mind, not carried away by fads; and it may help to be a slow, deep thinker rather than a brilliant, facile one. If the young writer is by nature a foolish person, his chances are bad, though perhaps, to tell the truth, not all *that* bad. Every teacher of middle age or more can count up instances of highly successful former students who, as freshmen or sophomores, even juniors or seniors, seemed silly beyond all hope of reclamation. People change, sometimes because of outside forces—sickness, a failed marriage, a shattering family death, sometimes love or success—sometimes from a gradual process of maturing and reconsideration.

As for the quality of strangeness, it is hard to know what can be said. There can be no great art, according to the poet Coleridge, without a certain strangeness. Most readers will recognize at once that he's right. There come moments in every great novel when we are startled by some development that is at once perfectly fitting and completely unexpected—for instance, the late, surprising entrance of Svidrigailov in *Crime and Punishment*, Mr. Rochester's disguise in *Jane Eyre*, the rooftop scene in *Nicholas Nickleby*, Tommy's stumbling upon the funeral in *Seize the Day*, the recognition moment in *Emma*, or those moments we experience in many novels when the ordinary and the extraordinary briefly interpenetrate, or things common suddenly show, if only for an instant, a different face. One has to be just a little crazy to write a great novel. One must be capable of allowing the darkest, most ancient and shrewd parts of one's being to take over the work from time to time. Or be capable of cracking the door now and then to the deep craziness of life itself—as when in *Anna Karenina* Levin proposes to Kitty in the same weird way Tolstoy himself proposed to his wife. Strangeness is the one quality in fiction that cannot be faked.

If I could explain exactly what I mean here, I could probably do what I think no one has ever done successfully: reveal the very roots of the creative process. The mystery is that even when one has experienced these moments, one finds, as mystics so often do, that after one has come out of them, one cannot say, or even clearly remember, what happened. In some apparently inexplicable way the mind opens up; one steps out of the world. One knows one was away because of the words one finds on the page when one comes back, a scene or a few lines more vivid and curious than anything one is capable of writing —though there they stand. (That experience, I suspect, is the motivating impulse behind the many stories of unearthly experiences confirmed in the final paragraph by some ring or coin or pink ribbon left behind by the otherworldly intruder.) All writing requires at least some measure of trancelike state: the writer must summon out of nonexistence some character, some scene, and he must focus that imaginary scene in his mind until he sees it as vividly as, in another state, he would see the typewriter and cluttered desk in front of him, or the last year's calendar on his wall. But at times—for most of us, all too occasionally—something happens, a demon takes over, or nightmare swings in, and the imaginary *becomes the real.*

I remember that once, writing the last chapter of *Grendel,* this altered sense of things came over me with great force. It was not at the time a new or surprising experience; the one respect in which it was odd was that after I came out of it I seemed to remember vividly what had happened. Grendel has just had his arm torn off and recognizes that he will die. He has stubbornly insisted throughout the novel that we have no free will, that all life is brute mechanics, all poetic vision a cynical falsehood, and he clings even now to those opinions, partly for fear that optimism is cowardice, partly from stubborn self-love: even though Beowulf has banged Grendel's head against a wall, bullying him into making up a poem about walls, Grendel is hanging on for dear life to his convictions, in terror of being swallowed by the universe and convinced that his opinions and his identity are one and the same. The "inspired" passage (I am of course not talking about its aesthetic value) begins approximately here:

> No one follows me now. I stumble again and with my one weak arm I cling to the huge twisted roots of an oak. I look down past stars to a terrifying darkness. I seem to recognize the place, but it's impossible. "Accident," I whisper. I will fall. I seem to desire the fall, and though I fight it with all my will I know in advance that I can't win. Standing baffled, quaking with fear, three feet from the edge of a nightmare cliff, I find myself, incredibly, moving toward it. I look down, down, into bottomless blackness, feeling the dark power moving in me like an ocean current, some monster inside me, deep sea wonder, dread night monarch astir in his cave, moving me slowly to my voluntary tumble into death.

Throughout the novel I'd made occasional allusions to the poetry and prose of William Blake, a major influence on my ideas about the imagination (its power to transform and redeem). Here, when I was simply following Grendel in my imagination, trying to feel in myself what it might be like to flee through deep woods, bleeding to death, I suddenly fell, without having planned it, into what I can only describe as a powerful dream of a Blakean landscape: the huge twisted roots of the oak, then a dizzying reversal of up and down (I had the sense of Grendel as fallen onto his back, looking up past the tree but imagining he was looking down, an image that recalls my childhood fear that if the planet is indeed round, I might one day fall off). Though the oak tree is from Blake, it was tinged in my mind with other associations. In Chaucer's poetry, with which I was then deeply involved, the oak is associated with Christ's cross and with sorrow in general; by another line it is associated with druids and human sacrifice, notions darkened for me by my childhood reaction to songs like "The Old Rugged Cross" (stained with blood so divine), grizzly and sickening reminders of beheaded chickens, butchered cows, child thoughts of death with undertones of guilt and the ultimate moral ugliness of God.

I did not, in my writing trance, separate these ideas out. I *saw* Blake's tree, exactly the same tree I saw when I read Chaucer's *The Book of the Duchess*, and its force was that of the cross I imagined in childhood, messy with blood and gobbets of flesh (an unorthodox image, I realize). I think, though I'm not sure, that it was this sense of the tree as tied to my childhood vision that made me react to it with a sense of déjà vu. Imitating (in fact feeling) Grendel's terror, I react in Grendel's way, clinging to my (his) opinion: "Accident!"—that is, Beowulf's victory has no moral meaning; all life is chance. But the fear that it may not all be accident strikes back instantly, prodded a little by childhood notions of the cross—blood, guilt, one's desperate wish to be a good boy, be loved both by one's parents and by that terrifying superfather whose otherness cannot be more frighteningly expressed than by the fact that he lives beyond the stars. So for all his conscious belief that it's all accident, Grendel *chooses* death, morally aligning himself with God (hence trying to save himself); that is, against his will he notices that he seems to "desire the fall." Abruptly the nightmare landscape shifts, from looking "down" past the tree into the abyss of night to another source of vertigo, looking down from the edge of a cliff. I did not consciously make this shift because of the nightmare I'd had in my sleep the night before I wrote this page; rather, I noticed as I made the shift that in fact what I was writing was a nightmare that I'd had and until that instant had forgotten.

A day or two before, my family and I had been watching Olympic ski jumpers practice—a terrifying business, to me at least, frightened as I am by heights. In a dream, the night before the writing of this passage, I'd found myself moving very slowly—but inexorably—toward the edge of the ski jump, the snow below me unspeakably far away. I'd felt in my nightmare, for whatever reason, exactly this same sense that I was willing the fall, in spite of myself. (I think there is some strange pun in the word "fall"; at any rate, it's a word I've often used elsewhere in its Edenic sense: so that the fear I felt as I was writing this passage—or enduring this entrancement— may have to do with moral paradox of the kind the unconscious takes wicked delight in: willing his death, Grendel is unconsciously trying to please God so that God will not slaughter him; willing "the Fall," he is defying the God he hates and fears.) Grendel feels the movement in himself to be in some way the movement of the universe. He is like "an ocean current," such a current as brought Beowulf to kill him; he feels that something inside him (his heart, his *id*) is at one with that current; and since earlier in the novel it was Grendel himself who lived "inside" (a cave), he is, since he houses the *id* monster, the mountain whose steeps he fears; he is some fabled mystery ("deep sea wonder"); and if the whole night sky is conceived as God's cave, then Grendel, "dread night monarch astir in his cave," is God. At the time I wrote the passage, I made all these connections (ocean current, monster, sea wonder, etc.) without consciously thinking: the mystical oneness, the calmly accepted paradox, were inherent in the entrancement.

The only point I mean to make out of this long and possibly self-indulgent analysis is this: All I myself know for sure, when I come out of one of these trance moments, is that I seem to have been taken over by some muse. Insofar as I'm able to remember what happened, it seems to me that it was this: for a moment the real process of our dreams has been harnessed. The magic key goes in, all the tumblers fall at once and the door swings open. Or: mental processes that are usually discrete for some reason act together. I was of course conscious, throughout my writing of *Grendel,* that what I was trying to talk about (or dramatize, or seek to get clear) was an annoying, sometimes painful disharmony in my own mental experience, a conflict between a wish for certainty, a sort of timid and legalistic rationality, on the one hand, and, on the other, an inclination toward childish optimism, what I might now describe as an occasional, flickering affirmation of all that was best in my early experience of Christianity. Surrounded by university people who had, as we say, "outgrown religion," and feeling uneasy about joining their party because to do so might be a cowardly surrender and a betrayal of my background, though refusing to do so might also be cowardice, and a betrayal of myself, I had gloomed through writers like Jean-Paul Sartre who seemed confident that they knew what they were talking about (I was not convinced); I'd joined churches and, finding them distasteful, had left; and I'd become, more or less by accident, a specialist in medieval Christian poetry, including of course *Beowulf,* source of, among other things, the quasi-mystical macrocosm/microcosm equations at the end of the passage I've been discussing. All the elements to be fused in the trance moment were in place, like the assembled components of the Frankenstein monster's body before the lightning strikes. What I can't really explain is the lightning. It may have to do with entering as fully as possible into the imaginary experience of the character, getting "outside" oneself (a paradox, since the character to be entered is a projection of the writer's self). It may have to do with the sense of mental strain one experiences at such moments: the whole mind seems tightened like a muscle, fierce with concentration. Anyway, if one is lucky the lightning strikes, and the madness at the core of the fictional idea for a moment glows on the page.

4

After verbal sensitivity, accuracy of eye, and a measure of the special intelligence of the storyteller, what the writer probably needs most is an almost daemonic compulsiveness. No novelist is hurt (at least as an artist) by a natural inclination to go to extremes, driving himself too hard, dissatisfied with himself and the world around him and driven to improve on both if he can.

A psychological wound is helpful, if it can be kept in partial control, to keep the novelist driven. Some fatal childhood accident for which one feels responsible and can never fully forgive oneself; a sense that one never quite earned one's parents' love; shame about one's origins—belligerent defensive guilt about one's race or country upbringing or the physical handicaps of one's parents—or embarrassment about one's own physical appearance: all these are promising signs. It may or may not be true that happy, well-adjusted children can become great novelists, but insofar as guilt or shame bend the soul inward they are likely, under the right conditions (neither too little discomfort nor too much), to serve the writer's project. By the nature of his work it is important that one way or another the novelist learn to depend primarily on himself, not others, that he love without too much need and dependency, and look inward (or toward some private standard) for approval and support. Often one finds novelists are people who learned in childhood to turn, in times of distress, to their own fantasies or to fiction, the voice of some comforting writer, not to human beings near at hand. This is not to deny that it also helps if a novelist finds himself with one or more loved ones who believe in his gift and work.

The novelist is in a fundamentally different situation from the writer of short stories or the poet. Generally speaking, if he wins, he wins more handsomely than they do: a commercially successful artistic novel—especially a third or fourth one —may bring in upwards of a hundred thousand dollars (no real win by businesspeople's standards; it may have taken him ten years to write) and in addition may bring stature, honor, maybe love letters from photogenic strangers. None of that is —or ought to be—the reason the novelist chose the genre he works in. He is the particular kind of writer he is, what William Gass has called a "big-breath writer," and in effect he does what is most natural for him. He has, unlike the poet or short story writer, the endurance and pace of a marathon runner. As Fitzgerald put it, there is a peasant in every good novelist. And he has, besides, the kind of ambition peculiar to novelists—a taste for the monumental. He may begin as a short story writer; most novelists do. But he quickly comes to find himself too narrowly caged: he needs more space, more characters, more world. So he writes his large book and, as I began by saying, if he wins, he wins handsomely. The trouble is (and this is the point I've been struggling toward), the novelist does not win nearly as often as do poets and writers of short stories. That is why he needs to be a driven man, or at any rate directed by inner forces, not daily or monthly bursts of applause. A good poem takes a couple of days, maybe a week, to write. A good short story takes about the same. A novel may take years. All writers thrive on praise and publication; the novelist is the writer who makes the huge, long-term investment, one that may or may not pay off.

A writer's successes bring him more than praise, publication, or money: they also help him toward confidence. With each success, writers, like stunt riders and ballet dancers, learn to dare more: they take on riskier projects and become more exacting in their standards. They get better. Here the novelist is at a disadvantage in comparison to writers of shorter forms. Especially in his apprentice years, when it matters most, success comes rarely.

Let us look more closely at the process a novelist must

depend upon. First of all, the serious novelist can seldom punch straight through, write from beginning to end, knock off a quick revision, and sell his book. The idea he's developing is too large for that, contains too many unmanageable elements —too many characters, each of whom the writer must not just create but figure out (as we figure out peculiar people in real life) and then must present convincingly; and the story contains too many scenes, too many moments, each of which the writer must imagine and render with all the intensity and care of his being. He may work for weeks, even months, without losing his focus and falling into confusion, but sooner or later —at least in my experience—the writer comes to the realization that he's lost. His overfamiliarity with the characters, after endless hours of writing and rewriting, may lead to his suddenly feeling bored with them, irritated by everything they say or do; or he may become so close to them that, for lack of objectivity, he's baffled by them. Just as we can often predict how casual acquaintances will behave in a given situation, though we cannot make out what we ourselves or those close to us would do, so writers often have a clearer fix on their characters when the novel is still a fresh idea than they do months later, when the writing is well along and the characters are like family. I myself am stopped cold when I cannot make out how a character would deal with the situation presented to him. If the situation presented is trivial, one's perplexity can be maddening. Once during the writing of *Mickelsson's Ghosts* I found the novel's heroine being offered an hors d'oeuvre, and I couldn't tell whether she would accept it or not. I forced the issue, made her refuse it; but then I found myself stuck. It didn't matter a particle which choice she made, but damned if I could move to the next sentence. "This is ridiculous," I told myself, and tried a little gin—to no avail. It seemed to me now that I knew nothing about this woman; I wasn't even sure she'd have come to the party in the first place. *I* wouldn't have. Stupidest party in all literature. I quit writing, put the manuscript away, and took out my frustration on woodworking tools, making furniture. A week or so later, in the middle of a band-saw cut, I saw, as if in a vision, the woman taking the hors d'oeuvre. I still didn't understand her, but I was positive I knew what she would do, and what she would do after that, and after that.

Or the novel may bog down because in terms of overall structure—pace, emphasis, and so on—the writer can no longer see the forest for the trees. I've often labored with ferocious concentration on a scene, polishing, revising, and tearing out; rewriting, polishing, and revising again until finally I realize that I have no idea what I'm doing, can't even recall why it was that I thought the scene necessary. Experience has taught me that, unpleasant as it is to do so, I have no choice but to put the manuscript away for a while—sometimes it takes months—and then look at it again. When the proper time has elapsed—in other words when the manuscript is "cold"—the faults stand plain. One may discover that the scene is much too elaborate in relation to scenes before and after it, or that it does not belong in the novel at all, or—this happened to me just once—that the scene is terrific but the rest of the novel has to go. It is hard even for an experienced writer to throw away two hundred pages of bad writing, or anyway it's hard if one is still close enough to the writing to remember how much time and work it took. A year or two later, taking a fresh look at those bottom-drawer pages, it is easy—even satisfying —to be merciless.

I think there really is no other way to write a long, serious novel. You work, shelve it for a while, work, shelve it again, work some more, month after month, year after year, and then one day you read the whole piece through and, so far as you can see, there are no mistakes. (The minute it's published and you read the printed book you see a thousand.) This tortuous process is not necessary, I suspect, for the writing of a popular novel in which the characters are not meant to have depth and complexity, where character A is consistently stingy and character B is consistently openhearted and nobody is a mass of contradictions, as are real human beings. But for a true novel there is generally no substitute for slow, slow baking. We've all heard the stories of Tolstoy's pains over *Anna Karenina*, Jane Austen's over *Emma*, or even Dostoevsky's over *Crime and Punishment*, a novel he grieved at having to publish prematurely, though he had worked at it much longer than most popular-fiction writers work at their novels.

So by the nature of the novelist's artistic process, success comes rarely. The worst result of this is that the novelist has a hard time achieving what I've called "authority," by which I do not mean confidence—the habit of believing one can do whatever one's art requires—but, rather, something visible on the page, or audible in the author's voice, an impression we get, and immediately trust, that this is a man who knows what he's doing—the same impression we get from great paintings or musical compositions. Nothing seems wasted, or labored, or tentative. We do not get the slightest sense that the writer is struggling to hear in his mind what he's saying, the rhythm with which he's saying it, and how it relates to something later in the book. As if without effort, he does it all at once. He snaps into the trance state as if nothing were easier. Probably only examples can suggest what I mean.

Notice the careful, tentative quality of the opening paragraph of Melville's *Omoo:*

> It was in the middle of a bright tropical afternoon that we made good our escape from the bay. The vessel we sought lay with her main-topsail aback about a league from the land, and was the only object that broke the broad expanse of the ocean.

There is, I think, nothing actively bad about this writing; but we get no sense of the speaker's character, no clear mood from the rhythm (we cannot tell how seriously to take the word "escape"), certainly no sense of prose invading the domain of poetry. If you're musical you will notice that the sentences fall naturally into $\frac{4}{4}$ time. That is:*

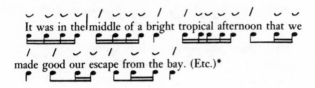

Compare what the same writer can do once he's found his booming, authoritative voice:

> Call me Ishmael. Some years ago—never mind how long precisely—having little or no money in my purse, and nothing particular to interest me on shore, I thought I would sail about a little and see the watery part of the world. . . .

That is what I mean by authority. No further comment is necessary, but notice how flowing, tricky, and finely balanced the music is. (Needless to say, another reader might analyze the rhythms differently. My notation reflects my own hearing of the sentences.)

$\frac{2}{4}$ Call me Ishmael. $\frac{4}{4}$ Some years ago—never mind how $\frac{2}{4}$ long precisely—

having $\frac{4}{4}$ little or no money in my purse, and nothing particular to

interest me on shore, I thought I would sail about a little and see the

watery part of the world. It is a way I have of driving off the spleen

and $\frac{2}{4}$ regulating the circulation . . . .

* ⌣ = unstressed syllable,
  / = stressed syllable (coinciding with the musical beat).

In *Omoo* the rhythms plod and dully echo each other:

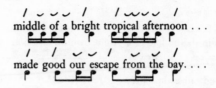

In *Moby Dick* the rhythms lift and roll, pause, gather, roll again. A few figures establish the basic pattern. For example, note the permutations of ♫ ♫♪:

Call me Ishmael

Some years ago

long precisely—having

nothing particular to

Etc.

Melville, we may be sure, did not sit down and score his rhythms like a composer, but his ear found them—found brilliantly subtle rhythmic variations, poetically functional alliteration (compare "broke the broad expanse of the ocean," in *Omoo*, with "watery part of the world. It is a way I have," in *Moby Dick*), and at the same time found orbicular rhetoric like a nineteenth-century congressman's or a Presbyterian minister's (as Mark Twain might say), and a compressed, energetic way of going for meaning. He reached authority.

Unlike a poet or short story writer a novelist cannot hope

to reach authority by frequent successes. I first declared myself a serious novelist in 1952, when I began *Nickel Mountain;* that is, I decided then that, come hell or high water, a novelist was what I would be. I published my first novel in 1966—not *Nickel Mountain.* I wrote several novels between 1952 and 1966, none of them successful even by my youthful standards. I worked, as I still work, long hours, seven days a week. As a young man I worked a regular eighteen-hour day; now I work less, but now I know more tricks and get more done in an hour. I do not mean to boast about this. Nearly all good novelists work as I do, and there are many good novelists in the world. (Besides, it can't really be called work. A famous basketball player once remarked, "If basketball were illegal, I'd be in prison for life." It's the same with novelists: they'd do what they do even if it were illegal, which, in comparison to basketball, it is.)

So—to return to the subject—a novelist is not likely to develop authority by success after success. In his apprenticeship years he succeeds, like Jack o' the Green, by eating his own white guts. He cannot help being a little irascible: some of his school friends are now rich, perhaps bemused by the fact that one of their smartest classmates is still struggling, getting nowhere, so far as anyone can see.

If the young would-be novelist is not in some way driven, he will never develop into a novelist. Most don't. Some give up, some get sidetracked. TV and film devour more brilliance and imagination than a thousand minotaurs. They need the true novelist's originality, but they cannot deal with it except in crippled form—pink slips instead of thought, and worse. I once visited a successful Hollywood producer, and he gave me a list of what "the American people don't like." They've done marketing research, and they know. The American people don't like movies with snowy landscapes. The American people don't like movies about farmers. The American people don't like movies in which the central characters are foreigners.

The list went on, but I stopped listening, because the movie I'd come to talk about concerned a Vietnamese immigrant family's first winter in Iowa. What one notices, when one hears about Hollywood marketing research, is that the only movie one is allowed to write is a cheap imitation of last year's blockbuster.

The would-be novelist can get sidetracked in many ways. He can do TV movies or "real" movies (this is not to deny that we occasionally get fine movies) or moronic TV episodes; he can become a full-time teacher of creative writing; he can move into advertising or porno or pieces for the *National Geographic*; he can become an interesting local bum; with a little popular-novel success he can become a regular on talk shows; he can become a politician or a contributor to *The New York Times* or the *New York Review of Books*. . . .

Nothing is harder than being a true novelist, unless that is all one wants to be, in which case, though becoming a true novelist is hard, everything else is harder.

Daemonic compulsiveness can kill as easily as it can save. The true novelist must be at once driven and indifferent. Van Gogh never sold a painting in his life. Poe came close with poetry and fiction, selling very little. Drivenness only helps if it forces the writer not to suicide but to the making of splendid works of art, allowing him indifference to whether or not the novel sells, whether or not it's appreciated. Drivenness is trouble for both the novelist and his friends; but no novelist, I think, can succeed without it. Along with the peasant in the novelist, there must be a man with a whip.

5

No one can really tell the beginning writer whether or not he has what it takes. Most people the young writer asks aren't qualified to judge. They may have impressive positions, even fame, but it's a law of the universe that 87 percent of all people in all professions are incompetent. The young writer must decide for himself, on the available evidence. I've given, in some detail, the evidence to think about:

Verbal facility is a mark of the promising novelist, but some great novelists don't have it, and some quite stupid novelists have it in abundance.

The accuracy and freshness of the writer's eye is of tremendous importance. But one can learn it if one hasn't got it. Usually. One can recognize that the abstract is seldom as effective as the concrete. "She was distressed" is not as good as, even, "She looked away."

Nothing is sillier than the creative writing teacher's dictum "Write about what you know." But whether you're writing about people or dragons, your personal observation of how things happen in the world—how character reveals itself—can turn a dead scene into a vital one. Preliminary good advice might be: Write as if you were a movie camera. Get exactly what is there. All human beings see with astonishing accuracy, not that they can necessarily write it down. When husbands and wives have fights, they work brilliantly, without consciously thinking. They go precisely as far as it's safe to go, they find the spouse's weakness, yet they know without thinking just when to hold back. The unconscious is smart. Writers have this brilliance in them as surely as do trout fishermen and mountain climbers. The trick is to bring it out, get it down. Getting it down precisely is all that is meant by "the accuracy of the writer's eye." Getting down what the writer really cares about—setting down what the writer himself notices, as opposed to what any fool might notice—is all that is meant by the *originality* of the writer's eye. Every human being has original vision. Most can't write it down without cheapening or falsifying. Most human beings haven't developed what Hemingway called the "built-in shock-resistant shit detector." But the writer who sets down exactly what he sees and feels, carefully revising time after time until he fully believes it, noticing when what he's saying is mere rhetoric or derivative vision, noticing when what he's said is not noble or impressive but silly—that writer, insofar as the world is just, will outlast Gibraltar.

As for the novelist's special intelligence, ask yourself whether or not you've got it. If you haven't, then knowing what it is may help you to develop it. If you dislike the novelist's special intelligence, don't become a novelist—unless, in spite of all I've said, you really want to.

Daemonic compulsiveness. If you haven't got it and you nevertheless write fine novels, I'll be the first to say, "Gentlemen, hats off!" I mention the value of compulsiveness because I would not have anyone go into the novelist's arena unarmed. There are many ways of surviving an activity not easily justified in practical terms. Thousands of Americans stand for hours in streams trying to catch fish. The novelist's work is no more visibly useless than amateur fish-catching. And I suspect most fishermen are not daemonically compulsive.

The question one asks of the young writer who wants to know if he's got what it takes is this: "Is writing novels what you want to do? *Really* want to do?"

If the young writer answers, "Yes," then all one can say is: Do it. In fact, he will anyway.

II.

THE WRITER'S TRAINING

AND EDUCATION

One of the most common questions asked by young writers is whether or not they should study creative writing and literature in college or graduate school. If the writer means only: "Will these courses help me become a better writer?" the answer is generally, Yes. If he or she means: "Will they improve my chances of supporting myself, for instance by getting a Master of Fine Arts degree and then getting a job teaching writing in college?" the answer is, Possibly. The world has far more writing teachers than it needs, and as a rule it is publication, not the MFA degree, that impresses employers, though an MA or MFA from a good school may help.

It's common for students to think of their college and/or grad school education in practical terms, as preparation for making a living. In many fields it is reasonable to think in this way, but not in the arts. European and English writers receive a good deal of support from the state, but in America, though federal, state, and local governments make feeble gestures of support (the whole National Endowment for the Arts comes to, I think, the cost of one frigate), it seems clear that nobody quite knows what to do with artists. In former times, when artists were church- or patron-supported, things were simple. Not now. Today, true, serious artists in all fields (music, visual arts, literature) are something like an alternative culture, a

73

group set apart from all other groups, from theology to professional pornography. They sacrifice the ordinary TV-watching pleasures of their society to pursue an ideal not especially valued by the society, and if they are lucky, they bring the society around, becoming culture heroes, but even the successful pay dearly. Both in the world of grants and in the marketplace, the novelist probably has a better chance than any other artist—certainly a better chance than the serious actor, poet, or composer. But very few novelists can support themselves by their writing. The study of writing, like the study of classical piano, is not practical but aristocratic. If one is born rich, one can easily afford to be an artist; if not, one has to afford one's art by sacrifice. On this, more later.

Let us turn to the benefits and dangers of going through a creative writing program and of studying literature in college.

It is true that most writers' workshops have faults; nevertheless, a relatively good writers' workshop can be beneficial. For one thing, workshops bring together groups of young writers who, even in the absence of superb teachers, can be of help to one another. Being with a group of serious writers at one's own stage of development makes the young writer feel less a freak than he might otherwise, and talking with other writers, looking at their work, listening to their comments, can abbreviate the apprenticeship process. It cannot be too strongly emphasized that, after the beginning stages, a writer needs social and psychological support.

When a writer first begins to write, he or she feels the same first thrill of achievement that the young gambler or oboe player feels: winning a little, losing some, the gambler sees the glorious possibilities, exactly as the young oboist feels an indescribable thrill when he gets a few phrases to sound like real music, phrases implying an infinite possibility for satisfaction and self-expression. As long as the gambler or oboist is only playing at being a gambler or oboist, everything seems possible. But when the day comes that he sets his mind on becoming a professional, suddenly he realizes how much there is to learn, how little he knows.

The young writer leaves the undergraduate college, where everyone agrees he is one of the best writers there, and he goes to, say, the Iowa Writers' Workshop, or Stanford, Columbia, or Binghamton. There he finds nearly every one of his classmates was a writing star at his or her college; he finds famous teachers who read his work and seem largely unimpressed; and suddenly the young writer's feelings are mainly alarm and disappointment. Why did his undergraduate teachers so mislead him? he wonders. I'm not sure myself why undergraduate reputations are inflated even by good teachers with high standards; perhaps because outside the specialized, nationally known writers' workshops one encounters relatively few young writers of real promise; or perhaps because at this early stage of a writer's work, the teacher believes that encouragement and praise seem more beneficial than a rigorous assessment of the writer's skills.

In any event, the writer adjusts (or else he gives up). He accepts the truth that he is not as great as his teachers and classmates imagined. He recognizes that the success he hopes for will take work. What a writer in this gloomy situation needs above all is a community that values what he values, a community that believes, rightly or wrongly, that it is better to be a good writer than to be a good executive, politician, or scientist. Good writers are after all intelligent people. They *could* have been executives, politicians, or scientists. They might not like or want such jobs, but they could do them, and in some ways any one of those jobs might be easier. What keeps the young writer with the potential for success from turning aside to some more generally approved, perhaps easier path is the writing community.

No doubt the truth is that as often as not the writing community saves the writer by its folly. It is partly made up of fools: young innocents who've not yet had the experience of valuing anything other than writing, and maniacs who, having considered other things, think writing the only truly valuable thing the human mind can do. It is partly made up of born writers: people who value other human activities but have no wish to do anything but write. (Asked why she wrote fiction, Flannery O'Connor once said, "Because I'm good at it.") Some members of every writing community are there because they're snobs: writing, or just being around writers, makes them feel superior; others are there because they think being a writer (though they may not have much talent) is romantic. Whatever their reasons or reasonings, these various contingents form, together, a group that helps the young writer forget his doubts. However good or bad the writing teacher, the young writer can count on close attention from all these kinds of people, not to mention a few chemists who enjoy going to readings. The young writer writes, feels uncertain about his work, and gets praise or, at very least, constructive criticism—or even destructive criticism, but from people who appear to care as much about writing as he does himself.

It's the same in all fields, of course. A young businessman in a society of people who can see only wickedness in business cannot easily remain a young businessman. We're social animals. Few born and bred Republicans remain Republicans in a context where everyone they know and respect is a Democrat. I've said that stubbornness is important for writers. But stubbornness can carry one only so far. If you grow up in a happy family and move to a community of pessimists—for example, if you grow up on a fortunate and peaceful farm in Indiana and move to New York City—you can stubbornly hold out, but only because you have, in your memory, something real to hold out for. (The same is true in reverse. Born and bred in Manhattan, you cannot easily shift to the less cynical attitudes of rural Ohio.) I don't mean to slight the complications. You may be by nature a pessimist, even though born to a happy family in Indiana. But in hostile circumstances

—that is, in the exclusive company of optimists—you cannot easily make art of your pessimism, you can only be odd and miserable.

So the first value of a writers' workshop is that it makes the young writer feel not only not abnormal but virtuous. In a writers' community, nearly all the talk is about writing. Even if you don't agree with most of what is said, you come to take for granted that no other talk is quite so important. Talk about writing, even in a mediocre community of writers, is exciting. It makes you forget that by your own standards, whatever they may be, you're not very good yet. It fills you with nervous energy, makes you want to leave the party and go home and write. And it's the sheer act of writing, more than anything else, that makes a writer.

On the other hand, the writer who avoids writers' workshops (or some other solid community of writers) is probably in for trouble. One can be fooled by the legend of, say, Jack London, and imagine that the best way to become a writer is to be a seaman or lumberjack. Jack London lived in an age when writers were folk heroes, as they are not now, and an age when technique was not quite as important as it is now. Though a tragic and noble man, he was a relatively bad writer. He could have used a few good teachers. Hemingway once remarked that "the best way to become a writer is to go off and write." But his own way of doing it was to go to Paris, where many of the great writers were, and to study with the greatest theorist of the time, and one of the shrewdest writers, Gertrude Stein. Joseph Conrad, though we tend to think of him as a solitary genius, worked in close community with Ford Maddox Ford, H. G. Wells, Henry James, and Stephen Crane, among others. Melville had Hawthorne and his circle. Great writers are almost always associated with a literary dynasty. It's hard to find an exception. (Incredibly, even Malcolm Lowry was part of a group.) So for psychological reasons, if for no other, even a bad workshop may be better than none.

If a bad writers' workshop is worth attending, a good one is more so. If I could, I would tell you what the good workshops are. Iowa, being the oldest and best known, always attracts good students and sometimes has fine teachers. Binghamton has a good program in fiction, which is why I teach there. I've already mentioned others I consider dependable—Columbia and Stanford; and the list might easily be expanded. But it's hard to give sure advice. For one thing, workshops change from year to year, as skillful writing teachers come and go; and for another, what makes a good workshop for one writer may be a disaster for another. I myself am not very interested in so-called experimental writing, though I do it sometimes and have occasionally been moved or delighted by works of fiction by William Gass (who does not normally teach writing) or Max Apple (with whom one can study at Rice). When I find I have in one of my writing classes a student who has no interest in the more or less traditional kind of fiction I favor, I know that both the student and I are in trouble. Much as I want to help him, I am the wrong kind of doctor. On the other hand, John Barth, who heads the writing program at Johns Hopkins and has gathered around him an interesting group of writers who, like himself, favor the new and strange, can have a crippling effect on the young realist. What all this suggests, of course, is that the student should select his writing program on the basis of its teachers, hunting out those whose interests seem closest to his own.

One of the things that make a good writers' workshop beneficial is that it has at least one or two brilliant students (also five or six solid, sensible ones, and then several who are either pretentious or ploddingly conventional). Even in the best writers' workshop one is likely to learn more from one's fellow students than from one's teachers. A workshop perceived to be better than most attracts good students, and because they are at the apprentice stage, these people can be counted on for careful scrutiny of one's work, for encouragement, and useful criticism. Teachers in the well-known workshops may or may not prove helpful. They tend to hire the more famous writers, but not all famous writers are good teachers. Moreover, the main commitment of famous writers is, as a rule, to their own work. However deeply they may care about their students, their main business is to work on a form that takes a great deal of time. Often their solution is to concentrate on the very best of their students and give the rest short shrift. There is no doubt, I think, that good teachers can be helpful to the young writer; but in practice it turns out that the student either encounters good writers who teach on the side and do not work as hard as they might at it, or good teachers who are not very good writers, so that what they teach is partly wrong, or good writers who cannot teach at all.

Whatever the quality of their teaching, famous writers do a good deal for writing programs. Perhaps the chief value of the famous writer is his presence, his contribution as a role model. Just by being around him day after day, the young writer learns how the famous man reads, and what he reads; how he perceives the world; how he relates to others and to his profession; even how he schedules his life. The famous writer's presence is vivid proof that the young writer's goal is not necessarily unreasonable. If the student is extraordinarily lucky, the famous writer may also be a good teacher: he not only knows what real art is but can explain it.

I must add that at some of the creative writing programs where I've visited or taught I've found excellent teachers who are not creative writers at all, really, though they may have published a story or two, or one novel years ago, or several mediocre novels. Some people can catch mistakes in student writing that they cannot see in their own, and some writers who have excellent minds write, by some quirk of personality, books unworthy of them. Sometimes the excellent writing teacher is a critic rather than a fiction writer; sometimes he is a person without literary credentials, perhaps a freshman English teacher who, drafted to teach a lower-level creative writing course, has proved to have a gift for it. How to find such teachers only luck or the grapevine can tell you. One can ask writers one admires where they would go if they were just starting out; or one can simply set out for a generally respected university and hope. The odds are good that one will find, in any major university, someone who can help.

One of the oddities of creative writing courses is that there exists no standard theory on how to teach creative writing. Many people ask—even some creative writing teachers—"Can writing really be taught?" No one asks that about painting or musical composition. Writing has been identified so strongly with "genius" or "inspiration" that people have tended to assume that the art cannot be passed on by such methods as the other arts have used. That perception may be partly right; the writing of fiction may be a less specific, detectable skill than painting or musicianship. But the reason for doubt that writing can be taught is also, I think, at least partly historical. From early times, schools of painting and music directly served religious and political functions in a way writing poetry or fiction did not. Since the church and city-state of Florence needed Giotto's skills, Giotto taught his methods; his near contemporaries Dante and Boccaccio worked, respectively, at politics and the teaching of literature. In any case, within the past twenty or thirty years, with the rise of creative writing programs in the United States, a pedagogy for the art has begun to develop, and with every passing year the general level of teaching improves. There are those who deplore this fact, claiming it as the main reason for the dreary sameness of so much of our fiction and poetry; and no doubt there is something to be said for that view. But at least at the technical level, it seems to me, fiction has never been better off. Probably the truth is that in any age there are only so many writers of genius, and teaching a writer not to make mistakes—teaching him to avoid those forms of vagueness or clumsiness that impair the vivid and continuous dream—cannot make him a more interesting or original person than he is. Perhaps the one great danger that the student in a good creative writing course ought to guard against is the tendency of good technical theory to undermine individuality and the willingness to take risks.

A bad workshop in creative writing has one or more regular features. If the student notices several of them in the workshop he has chosen, he should drop the course.

In a bad workshop, the teacher allows or even encourages attack. It is common in writers' workshops for the student to read a story (usually one he's gone over beforehand with the teacher), then get comments from his teacher and classmates. In a good workshop, the teacher establishes a general atmosphere of helpfulness rather than competitiveness or viciousness. Classmates of the writer whose work has been read do not begin, if the workshop is well run, by stating how *they* would have written the story, or by expressing their blind prejudices on what is or is not seemly; in other words, they do not begin by making up some different story or demanding a different style. They try to understand and appreciate the story that has been written. They assume, even if they secretly doubt it, that the story was carefully and intelligently constructed and that its oddities have some justification. If they cannot understand why the story is as it is, they ask questions. A common fault poor teachers inculcate in students is the habit of too quickly deciding that what they have failed to understand makes no sense. It takes confidence and good will to say, "I didn't understand so-and-so," rather than, belligerently, "So-and-so makes no sense." It is the nature of stupid people to hide their perplexity and attack what they cannot grasp. The wise admit their puzzlement (no prizes are given in heaven for fake infallibility), and when the problem material is explained they either laugh at themselves for failing to see it or they explain why they couldn't reasonably be expected to understand, thus enabling the author to see why he didn't get his point across.

Good workshop criticism, in other words, is like good criticism anywhere. When we read what is generally acknowledged to be a great work of art, we try to understand, if we have sense, why intelligent people, including the writer, have thought the work aesthetically satisfying. In a good fiction workshop one recognizes that even if a work seems bad at first glance, the writer sat writing and thinking about it for a fair amount of time and deserves a generous response. It is true, of course, that some of the fiction one hears read in a workshop is bad, and often there is no real question about its badness. The story is patently melodramatic, vague, pretentious, inadequately thought out, overloaded with detail, sentimental, uninterestingly vulgar. I myself think really bad fiction should never reach a reading in the workshop; it cannot teach much or sharpen students' critical skills, and it is likely to embarrass the writer. If bad fiction does reach the workshop, it should be dealt with quickly and politely, its mistakes made clear so that neither that writer nor any other in the workshop is inclined to repeat them, and its virtues acknowledged. But in most fiction that reaches workshop reading, the badness is not so obvious. The business of the teacher and the writer's classmates is to figure out (or if necessary ask) the purpose and meaning of the piece and only then to suggest carefully, thoughtfully, why the purpose and meaning did not come through.

A writer does not become better by being scorned. It is helpful if a class, as it listens to a writer's story, makes careful notes of apparent mistakes or weaknesses and reads them to the writer after the story has been read, but it is helpful only if the class generally understands that anyone's work could have similar shortcomings. If a class regularly attacks its members, and the teacher allows it, the course is counterproductive. The only final value of class criticism is that it teaches each member of the class to criticize and evaluate his own work and appreciate good fiction different from his own. Often class criticism can show the writer that he has at some specific point written misleadingly or has failed to evoke some important element of a scene—mistakes the writer could not catch himself because, knowing what he intended, he thinks his sentences say more than they do. He may imagine, for instance, that the bulge in his female character's coat clearly indicates that she is carrying a gun, whereas a listener not privy to the writer's mental image may imagine that the woman is pregnant. Seeing the effects of his mistakes makes the writer more careful, more wary of the trickery words are capable of. Or again, class criticism may make a writer aware of his unconscious prejudices, for instance his notion that fat people are easygoing, or that all hellfire fundamentalists are mean, or that all homosexuals try to seduce boys. The wide range of opinion a class affords increases the writer's chance of getting a fair hearing—especially the writer whose style, goals, and attitudes differ radically from his teacher's—and the focus of the whole class on the writer's work increases the odds that most of his mistakes or ineffective strategies will be noticed. At its best, class criticism can help everyone involved, as long as that criticism is basically generous. Vicious criticism leads to writer's block, both in the victim and in the attacker.

In a bad workshop, the teacher coerces his students into writing as he himself writes. The tendency is natural, though not excusable. The teacher has worked for years to figure out his style and has persistently rejected alternatives. The result is that if he is not careful he is likely to be resistant to writing markedly unlike his own or, worse, written in a style opposed to his own, as in the case of the elegant stylist confronting a rough, demotic prose. The teacher's purpose ought to be to help students find their *own* way. This is the point teacher and poet Dave Smith is making when he says, "My object is to catch right now what will embarrass my students when they look at their poetry ten years from now." His object, in other words, is not to impose some strictly personal standard but to notice, within the implicit laws of the student poet's standards, what will not stand up in time. The poetry teacher who by force turns a light, anapestic, lyrical poet into an ode writer in stern Anglo-Saxon rhythms, the fiction teacher unwilling to tolerate experimental writing of a kind he himself hates to read —the teacher who consciously or unconsciously seeks to make fundamental changes in his student's personality—is, at least for that student, an inadequate if not a destructive teacher.

In another kind of bad workshop, there are no standards of goodness. I mentioned earlier one common set of standards for good fiction—creation of a vivid and continuous dream, authorial generosity, intellectual and emotional significance, elegance and efficiency, and strangeness. Another teacher of writing may have other aesthetic values—though I hope most teachers would admit the general validity of these. If the teacher has no basic standards, his class is likely to develop none, and their comments can only be matters of preference or opinion. Writers will have nothing to strive toward or resist, nothing solid to judge by. As I've said, undue rigidity can be destructive; but even a rigid set of standards, if it's clear and at least more or less valid, can be useful in giving the student something to challenge. An individual style is developed as much by resistance as by emulation. Students of a teacher who refuses to set standards are in danger of falling into the philistine persuasion that all literary success is luck or public whim. In that class, the student who writes an excellent story about fishermen and dolphins will be open to the objection that some particular classmate hates all stories of the sea. This is not to say that standards cannot change, adapting themselves to new successes. The moment I propound my principles, I can count on it that some clever student will consciously, perhaps even brilliantly, defy them. In that case, as a serious teacher I must determine without guiding rules—nothing but my honest thought and emotions—whether or not the story works, that is, interests me and moves me. The workshop teacher who has no basic theory, no set of aesthetic values conscientiously worked out, is probably doomed to mediocrity, as is his class. There is in the end no substitute for a critical understanding of fiction—which is not to claim that fiction is philosophy.

No experienced teacher underestimates how hard it is to see a student's work in its own terms. Since I generally teach fairly advanced courses, mainly graduate school level, I've often seen student work I thought to be quite bad and then later learned that the same piece was singled out for praise or even publication by other teacher-writers I respect. Recently I was given a story (a work sample on the basis of which I was to decide whether or not the student should be admitted to my course) that had been praised by two earlier writing teachers, both of them firmly established writers reputed to be good teachers. I did admit the student; the energy and vividness of the work were undeniable. But I thought the story execrable. It was a first-person story told inside the head of a madman, a tour de force of violence and scatology, seething with malice, frighteningly cynical, ending in the same place it began. It did none of the things I think art ought to do, except that it was vivid and (in a nasty, discomforting way) interesting. And the sentences were carefully made. When I said, with restraint, that I did not like the story very much, the student sighed and confessed that he didn't like it, either. Some of the verbs were too low-key, he said, and when he tried to put in more lively verbs they seemed to call undue attention to themselves. At this point, of course, I saw that I hadn't been thinking well. The student really was a gifted writer, fully conscious of what he was doing, earnestly looking for help from a teacher whose standards are about as applicable to his project as the rules of pinochle or the gladiator's oath.

One forgets the extent to which aesthetic standards are projections of one's own personality, defensive armor, or wishful thinking about the world. If there are objective laws of aesthetics, not all of them apply in every instance, and none of them finally have to do with purpose. One can argue, as I've done elsewhere, that—descriptively speaking—the fiction that lasts tends to be "moral," that is, it works with a minimum of cynical manipulation and it tends to reach affirmations favorable rather than opposed to life. One can argue on this basis that a writer is generally unwise to fake despair and nihilism he does not really feel. One cannot argue that the writer's purpose should be the creation of moral fiction, or any other kind; one cannot even argue that his purpose should be to create something beautiful or pleasing or even honest or universally interesting. A given writer may wish to set such standards for his students; but insofar as he means to be a teacher, he must leave room for intelligent rebellion.

In a bad workshop, the teacher takes the place of the student's critical imagination. This is the one great danger in a workshop where the teacher is not only an impressive writer but also a skillful and articulate teacher, one who can figure out narrative or stylistic problems, solve them, and make his mental processes clear to students. This fully articulate teaching implies, of course, a close teacher-student relationship—not just one in which the teacher jots an occasional comment on the student's writing but rather one in which the teacher goes over each of the student's works with meticulous care, missing neither the virtues of the piece nor the defects. How it is that the best teacher's help and concern can impede the student's progress—how the virtue of showing students ways of evaluating and correcting their fiction can pass over into the defect of making student minds clones of the teacher's—is a matter both teacher and student need to become sensitive to.

The best kind of writing teacher, it seems to me, not only meets his regular workshop classes but deals with each student individually, half an hour or an hour each week or so, in tutorial sessions, like a violin instructor. The teacher closely analyzes the student's work and shows him, not on the basis of the teacher's own personal preferences but in terms of the inherent logic of the student's fiction, what is right and wrong and what needs to be done. This is not a matter of opinion or individual feeling. In any true story, certain things have to be shown dramatically, others can be summarized or implied. In general the rule is simply this: Anything necessary to the action's development must be shown dramatically. For instance, if a man is to beat his dog, it is not enough for the writer to *tell* us that the man is inclined to violence or that the dog annoys him: we must see how and why the man inclines to violence, and we must see the dog annoying him. For young writers it is sometimes hard to recognize what has to be dramatized or how it can be done. And here the problem arises.

Nothing is easier than to give the student specific actions, even specific sentences, that will solve his story's problems; and at a certain point in the young writer's development it may perhaps be valuable to do such things, so that the student can get the hang of it. But basically what teachers need to teach students is not how to fix a particular story but how to figure out what is wrong with the story and how to think about alternative ways of fixing it. At the Bread Loaf Writers' Conference I've frequently worked with writing assistants—young writers with successful first novels—whose inexperience as teachers led them to focus on finding the best solution to problems in the writing placed in their care, led them, in other words, to show the student writer what to do to make his fiction work. In case after case, when I myself looked at the student's work later, I felt there were a number of possible solutions to the problems—alternative solutions whose relative value must depend on the student writer's preferences—and that in suggesting only one solution, the one he himself would choose, my assistant had done an unwitting disservice to the student. What the beginner needs to learn is how to think like a novelist. What he does not need is a teacher who imposes his own solution, like an algebra teacher who tells you the answer without showing how he got there, because it is *process* that the young writer must learn: problems in novels, unlike problems in algebra, may have any number of solutions. At some point —the sooner the better, some would say—the teacher's job is simply to say, "Not good enough," and vanish.

Finally, a bad fiction workshop is "workshoppy." It tends to emphasize theme and design over feeling and authentic narrative. Working too much with too many young writers, or having no teaching talent in the first place, the teacher may slide into simplifying his work by forcing original ideas into what all good editors immediately recognize as workshop formulas. The evil is perhaps most easily described in the case of poetry: rather than helping the student poet to feel out the natural development of his poem, the writing teacher may rest on some simpleminded habit of design—for instance, the notion of "orchestration," the idea that the end of a poem should somehow bring back, like a musical comedy, all its main ideas and images in a final stanza. The same mistake is possible in fiction. Beware of the teacher who cries, "Reprise! Reprise!" The reader who encounters a reprise ending—if he's not very good at reading poetry or fiction—feels a superficial thrill of recognition. The more experience he gets, the more annoyed he is by such foolishness.

A story may be "workshoppy" because the writer (or the teacher) has too often thought from the literature student's point of view rather than from the writer's, so that instead of working like a storyteller, beginning with what happens and why, and only gradually moving (in his thought process if not in the actual writing) to the larger issues (how this story is in some way every human story, an expression of a constant or universal theme), the student writer begins with theme, symbolism, etc., in effect working backward from his imagined New Criticism analysis of a story not yet in existence. One can quickly spot this tendency in a workshop. Class discussion of a story begins in the wrong place, not with the immediate virtues of good fiction (an interesting and original but not distracting style, a clear and well-designed plot, vivid characterization and setting, an interesting and expressive use of a particular genre) but with the kinds of things normally central to a class in literature (theme and symbol). It is of course true that in a given story these less immediate matters may be the appropriate starting point; indeed, one mark of the first-rate writing teacher is his ability to move discussion swiftly to what happens to be the most important ground for judgment of the story at hand.

Another reason workshops become "workshoppy" is that often teachers slide unconsciously into overprizing the kind of narrative writing that teaches well, undervaluing and even dismissing work that does not. This sometimes gives an advantage to, for instance, the symbolic or allegorical story over the straightforward, well-crafted realistic story, and to almost any short story over the more sprawling prose of a novel-in-progress. For the teacher, a well-made allegorical story is a delight, a puzzle he and the class can, if they wish, play with for hours. In the fiction workshop I am teaching this semester I encountered a story entitled "Jason," which I hope soon to publish in the magazine I edit, *MSS*. Early in the story, a child, Jason, loses one shoe; much later in the story, we come to a huge old Vermont inn, many-storied and circular, whose hallways wrap around like the coils of a snake (the idea is better expressed in the original). The story is told so cunningly, with such realistic detail, that only one member of this well-read graduate class caught on to the writer's use of the Jason and Medea myth. Once the secret was out, the class pounced on one allusion after another, and after that members of the class delighted in turning over, with subtlety almost equal to the writer's, the story's deconstructionist (or revisionist) tricks. I think no one who attended the class or has read the story would deny that it's an interesting and effective piece. But the point is, the first chapter of Tolstoy's *Anna Karenina* probably could not have stirred such lively discussion.

Short fiction in the symbolic or allegorical mode can no

more compete in the arena of well-constructed full-length novels than a bantamweight can hope to compete in the ring with a skillful heavyweight. (It goes without saying that each has its/his place.) But in the writers' workshop the heavyweight may not fare well. For practical reasons (the fact that young novelists try out their wings on the short story, for one thing), most creative writing workshops are oriented toward short fiction. For the young novelist, this can be troublesome. His talent may go unnoticed: his marathon-runner pace does not stir the same interest as the story writer's sprinter's pace; and the kinds of mistakes workshops focus on are not as important in a novel as in a short story. Poets and short story writers must learn to work with the care of a miniaturist in the visual arts. Novelists can afford to stand back now and then and throw paint at the wall. Granted, they must throw well; but there can be no comparison between the skillful paint thrower and the Japanese master who touches his brush to the surface between heartbeats. Sometimes it happens that the young novelist distorts his art in an attempt to compete with the short story writers in his class. He tries to make every chapter zing, tries dense symbolism and staggeringly rich prose; he violates the novelistic pace.

Ideally, he belongs in a novel-writing workshop. The young novelist is as different from the young short story writer as the young short story writer is from the poet. The aesthetic problems he must work out are different from those that confront the story writer, and the novelist's whole character and way of working are different. (Granted, some people write both good novels and good short stories. I am speaking of extreme examples of the two types of writer.) Every three or four years I run a novel workshop (the rest of the time I teach workshops for anyone who wants to come and can already write well enough to get in). The novel workshop is, one soon learns, serious business. The people who become my students wait like hill-country outlaws for the course to be given, and then, when it is finally announced, strike like snakes.

In the last workshop I gave I had ten students. I asked that they work up a novel outline, which we would go over in class, and then that they present me, each week after that, with a new chapter and also a revision of the former chapter (revised in the light of our conference discussion of it). I didn't believe anyone could really hold to this schedule; I presented it only as an ideal to work toward, pointing out that the farther they were able to get on their novels, the more I would be able to show them about episode rhythm, overall construction, and so on. All but one of the students kept to the schedule. The exception, a town woman with a full-time job, was hospitalized as a result of overwork. I pushed these students no harder than I push students in other workshops. (In fact, I hardly push at all. If the student doesn't feel like writing, I don't have to read his work.) The novelists pushed themselves, as novelists characteristically do. The true young novelist has the stamina, patience, and single-mindedness of a draft horse. Those novel-workshop students who were involved with other college courses that semester dropped those other courses. Of the ten students in the course, eight later published their novels.

Students like these have no very comfortable place in the elegant, leisurely world of poets and short story writers. In the usual creative writing course, the potentially fine young novelist may even look rather dull. One of the best young novelists I ever taught, now a successful writer, got bad grades in high school and entered college (as a rugby player) with one of the lowest verbal aptitude scores on record at that university. His grammar was awful and his social adjustment was less than might have been desired. He stands for me as a kind of symbol of the young novelist, even though some are in fact witty, classy, and petite.

You know you're in a good writers' workshop if nearly everyone in the class is glad to be there, if writing and talk about writing become, in the course of the term, an increasingly exciting business, and if the writers in the workshop become increasingly effective as writers. The chief mark of a bad writing class is teacher meanness. Beware of the teacher who scoffs at "little magazines," claiming that they promote and proliferate mediocrity: you are dealing with a snob. Beware of the teacher who loves little magazines and hates *Esquire*, *The New Yorker*, or the *Atlantic*. You are looking at the same snob in drag. If you feel miserable in your writers' workshop, you should talk about your misery in private with the teacher, and if things don't improve, you should quit. A bad writing class doesn't only fail to teach writing, it can make one give up.

It is of course possible to become a good writer without a college education or, more specifically, without courses in literature. One does not have to be college-educated to be a sensitive and intelligent human being; in fact, there are some advantages to remaining one of the so-called common people, and thus avoiding the subtle social distancing higher education imposes. Writing ability, however improvable by teaching, is in large part a gift. If one cannot get to college, one need not despair of being a writer.

On the other hand, a college education gives advantages not to be lightly dismissed. The uneducated writer may successfully tell the stories of the people around him, may set down their longings and sufferings in comic or deeply moving or awe-inspiring ways; and if he is a self-educated writer, one who reads books, goes to good movies, and listens intently to the stories he hears among his friends and fellow workers, he may even become a subtle and original storyteller. But he will almost certainly remain a sort of primitive, that is, a kind of folk writer; he has difficulty becoming a virtuoso, one of those writers whose fictions impress us not only by their truth to life but also by their brilliance, their value as performance.

It's hard to explain the difference between a well-educated writer, one who understands from inside the beauty of a play by Shakespeare, the strange genius of James Joyce, Andrei Bely, or Thomas Mann, and an equally intelligent writer who knows only "the world" or, at best, knows only the world and the popular books he can get from his local drugstore, from a book club, or at a nearby branch of Waldenbooks. The uneducated writer is, for one thing, locked in his own time and place. Not knowing (not really knowing) about Homer or Racine or the contemporary fiction of South America, not knowing the many different ways in which a story can be told, from the rough-hemp tale-spinning of the saga poets to the dandified French allegorical tricks of the Middle Ages to the strange ways of India and China or avant-garde contemporary Africans, Poles, or Americans, he is like a carpenter with only a few crude tools: a hammer, a knife, a drill, a pair of pliers. He has no knowledge of the cunning tools of other times and places, with the result that when he asks himself what the best way of telling a given story might be, he has only two or three answers available. Or to put it another way, he has very few models for his work. He may use superbly the models he knows, becoming the literary equivalent of a maker of fine Shaker chairs; but what he might have done had he known other ways and means we will never find out.

What the writer should study if he goes to college is debatable. A good program of courses in philosophy, along with creative writing, can clarify the writer's sense of what questions are important—in other words, what worries and obsessions may give real importance to the writer's fiction. There are obvious dangers. Like any other discipline, philosophy is apt to be inbred, concerned about questions any normal human being would find transparently ridiculous. If one reads major journals on aesthetics, for instance, one cannot help but notice that most of the people who write about the arts seem never to have noticed how the arts really work. With solemn jargon and diagrams, professional aestheticians seek to demonstrate that fiction does or does not actually arouse feelings in the reader; or with great shows of learning they seek to demonstrate that fiction does or does not have, in any real sense, "meaning." All human thought has its bullshit quotient, and professional thought about thought has more than most. Nevertheless, the study of philosophy, perhaps with courses in psychology thrown in, can give the young writer a clear sense of why our age is so troubled, why people of our time suffer in ways different from the ways in which people of other times and places suffered. Though the ordinary housewife, politician, or ballplayer, as well as most academics, may never have read Nietzsche, Wittgenstein, or Heidegger, the ideas of those philosophers help make clear—or helped to cause—the problems of ordinary modern people. Moreover, for a certain kind of writer philosophy is interesting in itself. Writers always write best about what they most care about. The writer who cares more about philosophy than about anything else (except writing) should study philosophy.

For another kind of writer, the most valuable course of study may be one of the hard sciences. This is especially true, obviously, of the serious writer whose chief literary love is sophisticated sci-fi. Though it is true that most science fiction is junk, some of it is excellent. Certain books spring immediately to mind—some of Ray Bradbury's work or Kurt Vonnegut's, certain modern classics like *Brave New World* and *1984*, not to mention works of obvious high-class intent, such as Thomas Pynchon's *Gravity's Rainbow*, William Burroughs's *The Ticket That Exploded*, or the work of major writers outside America, like Kobo Abe, Italo Calvino, Raymond Queneau, or Doris Lessing. The number of aesthetically valuable works of science fiction is greater than the academy generally notices. One finds intelligence and emotional power in, for instance, Walter Miller's *A Canticle for Leibowitz* (mentioned earlier), the fiction of Samuel R. Delaney, some of Robert

Silverberg, Roger Zelazny, Isaac Asimov, and, when he holds in the fascism, Robert Heinlein. One finds a fair measure of literary merit in Algis J. Budrys's *Michaelmas* or the work of Robert Wilson, whose novels (for instance, *Schrodinger's Cat*) out-Barth John Barth without sacrificing the primary quality of good fiction, interesting storytelling. And science fiction is the domain of one of the greatest living writers, Stanislaw Lem.

I don't mean to say that a scientific background needs to lead the writer to science fiction. Many writers—Walker Percy and John Fowles, for example—put their scientific knowledge to work in writing fiction of the here and now, thereby enriching their art. More and more, as we look around, we see science and literature coming together—Nabokov's moths, Updike's symbolism drawn from, among other sciences, astronomy and botany, Philip Appleman's Darwin poems, and so on. As twentieth-century science becomes increasingly the basis of our life metaphors—relativity, uncertainty, entropy, infinite transformation—and as technology becomes the very ground we stand on, whether we live in skyscrapers or on space stations, a background in science looks better and better as a springboard into writing. A science background cannot help the writer develop the literary skills that change an ordinary work into a fine one, but like any other discipline, it can give the young novelist, insofar as he cares about that discipline, important subject matter.

I will not go on to discuss the advantages and disadvantages of studying the social sciences, history or law, and so forth. A good writer may come out of any intellectual discipline at all. Every art and science gives the writer its own special ways of seeing, gives him experience with interesting people, and can provide him with means of making a living—supporting himself while he writes. Since only a few novelists, including very good ones, earn enough by their fiction to take care of themselves and their families, and since after a day of hard manual labor or taxing white-collar office stress it is hard to sit down and write fiction, the young novelist is wise to train himself in some profession where, if he likes, he can ease up a little, take some of his time for writing. Some novelists (Al Lebowitz) practice law part-time; some (Frederick Buechner) are ministers; some are doctors (Walker Percy); a great many are teachers. The trick, of course, is to find a profession you like and one that will also feed your writing, and not eat up all your time.

It is not necessary—or perhaps not even advisable—that the young writer major in literature. It *is* advisable that he take as many good literature courses as he's able to work in. Only the close study of the great literature of the past, in whatever language, can show the writer clearly what emotional and intellectual heights are possible. And only the study of literature can awaken the writer to those techniques which, if he reads only modern literature, he would never know the existence of. Very good young writers invariably become so by exposing themselves to good models, usually by getting a good teacher's help as they explore fiction of the far and near past. Sooner or later they learn the techniques of the so-called New Criticism (expressed in such books as *Understanding Fiction*, by Cleanth Brooks and Robert Penn Warren, *Reading Modern Short Stories*, by Jarvis Thurston, or *The Forms of Fiction*, by Lennis Dunlap and John Gardner; more recent books, such as *Fiction 100*, 2nd Edition edited by J. Pickering, give less emphasis to close analysis but tend to achieve the same thing, an ability to read closely). Learning to read a literary text well helps the student create more complex and interesting fiction. Insofar as possible, the young writer should choose courses dealing with the greatest literary figures available. And he should never study what he can easily figure out on his own. Most survey literature courses, by this rule, should be avoided.

Whatever the student majors in, and whatever he selects for elective courses, college work is enriching, probably more stimulating than anything else the young person can do at this period of his life. If he can, the young writer should give at least glancing attention to as many as possible of the major fields of study: a foreign language, history, philosophy, psychology, one or more of the hard sciences, fine arts. Glancing attention to these fields will enable the student to pursue them further on his own whenever he—or one of his characters—needs information. After his undergraduate years, the young writer who has played the field will find himself drawn naturally to additional interests, picking up paperback books about UFOs, botany, or the Russian Revolution, or falling into intense conversation, at parties, with morticians, go-go dancers, and dog trainers. Even a weak education opens up new worlds. Most writers, one may as well admit, get weak educations. Their minds are too much on their writing, and they lack proper respect. The writer ought not to be too proud of this. At the very least, he should learn to spell.

III.

PUBLICATION

AND SURVIVAL

Some writing teachers claim that the student writer should never think about publishing but should simply work hard at learning his craft—presumably on the assumption that if the student learns his craft well enough, publication will take care of itself. The assumption is probably right, but I'm suspicious of those who argue it: I suspect the teacher's main motive is the wish not to be bugged by students about publication. And in any case, though it's generally true that one ought not to publish until one has work worth publishing, and that when one does have such work, publication is not likely to prove inordinately difficult, it is nevertheless a fact of life that young writers do want to get published, and to tell them "Hush and eat your spinach" is to evade real problems.

Young writers want to publish because they're unsure of themselves. However talented they may be, they cannot go on writing for long (as a rule) without some reassurance beyond their fellow students' praise and the teacher's A minus. Part of the good young writer's virtue is his wish that "real" people like his work—some editor who does not know him, some casual reader in Lost Nation, Iowa. It is perhaps unreasonable to ask the writing teacher to make a special effort to get his competent students published; he has enough to do already— far more than the ordinary teacher of literature, who can meet his classes, grade two or three sets of papers a term, and spend the rest of his time fishing. (I speak as a teacher who has done both.) But the teacher should at least recognize that the student's wish is legitimate and healthy; and if the student's work really is good enough to publish, the teacher ought not to scorn the student's wish. Some widely respected writing teachers— for instance, the novelist Robert Coover—are famous for the energy and relative success with which they push their students' work on appropriate editors. Since students need confidence to write at all, and respectable publication is one of the roads to confidence, the teacher does well to offer what help or encouragement he can.

More important, of all the hard things a student needs to learn in order to become a professional writer, nothing is more self-preserving than learning the ropes of publication, so he might as well start learning while still in school. In some ways the young writer may need as much guidance in the matter of publication as he needs in the development of writing skills. Letters of rejection from even the most respectable magazines may be wise and helpful but are more likely to be perfunctory. I have seen editors complain of "too obvious symbolism" in a story no one else would call symbolic, and recommend cutting what any sane reader would instantly recognize as the best moment in the story. The editor may complain of sentimentality in a story I myself would call not sentimental but authentically moving; or he may, after skimming a story too quickly, complain that the plot is unclear, though in fact it's clear as day. Getting any letter at all from an editor is of course a mark of interest—it shows he thinks too much of the writer to send out a printed rejection slip—but the writer must learn not to take such letters of rejection too seriously. For the young writer, that is a hard thing to learn. The editor has power; surely he's smart. And the editor liked the story enough to send a letter; perhaps with just a few changes—even if they seem senseless —he'll accept the story and print it.

The writer sends out, and sends out again, and again and again, and the rejections keep coming, whether printed slips or letters, and so at last the moment comes when many a promising writer folds his wings and drops. His teachers and classmates praised him, back in school, his spouse is baffled by the rejections; but the writer's despair wins out. It's a terrible thing to write for five or even ten years and continue to be rejected. (I know.) And so at last, down goes another good writer. (Let no one tell you that all good writers eventually get published.) At this precarious moment when he's ready to give up, the writer needs three things: trustworthy reassurance that his work really is of publishable quality; a clear understanding of how editing works, so that the editor's damage to the writer's ego is minimized; and the strongest possible support from teachers and friends. It will not hurt, of course, if he can get one thing more: a contact—some writer or agent or famous critic who can help. Let me pause a moment on these three things, or rather four, that the young writer needs as he approaches his hour of despair.

Most rejected fiction is rejected because it's not good. Not all is rejected for this reason, as I've said: some is rejected because it was sent to the wrong kind of publisher, or because it never got past the slush-pile reader, who's tired and maybe not too bright, or because the publisher has a backlog, or because the editor cannot stand stories about cows. But most rejected fiction is rejected because it's bad. The writer, in this case, needs to find a better teacher, or if he can't get a teacher he should study the various books about writing—though for the writer who's worked for years and is still just plain bad, neither courses nor manuals are likely to help.

Sometimes good writing gets rejected by the very editor who ought to have recognized its worth. One should fight like the devil the temptation to think well of editors. They are all, without exception—at least some of the time—incompetent or crazy. By the nature of their profession they read too much, with the result that they grow jaded and cannot see new talent though it dances in front of their eyes. Like writers, they are under insupportable pressures: they have to choose books that will sell, or at least bring the publisher honor, so they become hypercritical, gun-shy, cynical. Often they are consciously or (more often) unconsciously guided by unspoken policies of the publishing house or magazine they work for. *The New Yorker*, for instance (to mention one of the best), has from the beginning been elegant and rather timid, a perfect magazine for selling expensive clothes and fine china, and its fiction editors, probably without knowing they do it, regularly duck from strong emotion or strong, masculine characters, preferring the refined and tentative. Alfred A. Knopf, one of the most respected publishers of novels, tends to resist publishing a profoundly pessimistic book. It is useful, in short, for young writers always to think of editors as limited people, though if possible one should treat them politely.

Understanding editors, one will recognize that at certain points one can stop thinking of them as enemies and begin to consider them friends. Although they're skittish and sometimes blind to real talent, they are often ambitious idealists; they would like nothing better than to discover and publish a great book—or even a moderately good one. This means they can be worked. They would *like* to publish a certain young writer's book, but they're unsure of themselves, so the thing for the young writer to do is win prizes and honors, fellowships and grants. If other people have admired the young writer, the editor feels more comfortable doing the same. (The editor is happiest when he can bet on a favorite while at the same time appearing to have discovered him.) Publication in one magazine makes publication in the next one much easier, as long as the writer is a good writer in the first place. And publication in several magazines—especially one or two reputedly good ones, like the *Georgia Review* or the *Atlantic* or *The New Yorker*

—increases the odds that when one is ready with a novel, it will be taken.

Once the editor has made up his mind to take a chance on the writer, some trick of the mind makes him sure he was right, and from that moment on, all the editor can see in the writer is good and more good. He may give advice, may even make annoying changes in the writer's manuscript, but essentially not even the writer's mother can love the writer as that editor does. He tells everyone he can find—his wife and children, his friends who write reviews, his fellow editors—and as the publication date nears, the editor's whole world, not to mention the writer's, begins to vibrate with panicky joy. If the writer is savaged by reviewers, the editor will be at least as angry as the writer, and the next book the writer sends in, the editor will fight for, partly because he likes it, partly because he has bet his credibility on the writer's career. Editors, at this point, are the bravest, most wonderful people on earth. A newly discovered writer has to go far out of his way—some writers do manage it—to turn his editor against him.

Let me pause for a few words on what the editors of novels do. Either by way of an agent (on which more in a moment) or "over the transom"—that is by direct submission from the writer—the novel arrives at the editor's desk. Normally a note comes with it, partly because mention of the writer's previous publications may help sway the editor (so the writer or agent hopes), and partly because sending a note is common politeness. If the note is from an agent, it is sure to address a particular editor by name, since a given book is likely to be of more interest to one editor than to another. The young novelist living in Filer, Idaho, or St. Joseph, Missouri, may have a hard time getting a specific editor's name and may have no idea which editor would like what. If so, "Dear Editor" will do, though obviously that writer would be better off with an agent. (Magazine submissions, like submissions to publishing houses, should also go, ideally, to a particular editor.)

As soon as he possibly can, depending upon how many manuscripts he's received that day or week, the editor reads the manuscript. At major publishing houses this is usually not a long-drawn-out process. Little-magazine editors are often not paid for their editorial work, have other responsibilities such as teaching, and in any case are so deluged with manuscripts they can't possibly be prompt; but at publishing houses the selection process is usually efficient. It may be, in a given house, that slush-pile readers cull out the obviously bad work, then pass on the better manuscripts to more senior people. One way or another, the better manuscripts reach a senior editor, who, as I've said, reads it fairly quickly and, in my experience, as conscientiously as he knows how. He thinks about various things as he reads, notably: Is this a book that is likely to sell or bring the house prestige? Is it the kind of book that's suitable to this particular house? (Publishers have various specializa- tions, and the editor who pushes for a book too far outside the specialization of the house knows he's running a number of risks. In a house where final decisions are made by an editorial committee—the usual case—he may lose his fight with the other editors. In smaller houses, where one or two senior edi- tors make the final decision, he may not only lose his fight for the book but also lose credibility with the boss or bosses. Or if he wins his fight for a book that is not within the usual range of his house, the sales force may misunderstand or fail to push the book. The salesmen for a publishing house have large districts to cover, a great many bookstore owners or managers to visit. Except in those rare cases—and they do occur—when the salespeople believe strongly in an unusual book, one that requires them to take extra time making a special presentation to the buyer, they tend to mention the unfamiliar book and, getting no reaction, hurry on. Editors, knowing this, do not often push hard for a book they believe most of the sales force will find an annoyance.) But the main thing the editor asks himself is: "Do I really *like* this book?" Experienced editors have a keen eye for what is, according to some standard (commercial or aesthetic), good. They are good readers; that is, when a novel ends disappointingly, or has lumpish spots, or will annoy readers in an unjustifiable way, they know it.

If a book is generally well written and intelligent (given its intended audience) but seems to the editor finally unsuccessful, the editor writes what he means to be (and what sometimes is) a thoughtful, helpful letter to the writer or his agent. He explains what he likes and what he doesn't like, where the book succeeds and where it fails. The writer who gets such a letter should understand that the editor is interested in his work (otherwise, of course, he'd fire off a printed rejection slip, or no comment at all). If the writer agrees with the editor's comments (after a suitable period of calming down, getting rid of his anger or depression), he is wise to revise his book and submit it again to the editor who signed the letter. If the writer doesn't agree, he should of course try elsewhere. The editor reads the resubmitted book and either decides to take it or sends further (or new) objections. Again, if the writer comes to feel that the editor is right, he should again revise and again resubmit. It is probably true that his odds are going down— he can gauge this by the tone of the second rejection letter. Sometimes when an editor rejects a book more than once, each time with a carefully reasoned letter, he's rejecting the book for reasons he's not fully conscious of. Nonetheless, as long as the editor's comments seem right to the writer, on due reflection, his best course is to keep revising. He may never convince this particular editor, but the writer is wise to take good advice wherever he can find it: as long as the editor is willing to keep commenting, he's of use. Writers often feel—especially writers prone to dejection—that repeated rejections accompanied by reasoned letters mean that in the end there's no hope. This is simply not true. All editors want to publish (within the boundaries of their profit requirements) excellent books, and they are willing to help the promising writer achieve those standards.

None of this is to say that the writer should make changes that he does not believe in. But he should make sure he has understood the objections. It is sometimes supposed that editors suggest changes in a good writer's book to make the book more commercial. In my experience this isn't true, and a recent questionnaire asking successful writers their opinion on the matter showed that their experiences are mostly like my own. If you write a thriller, the editor will try to make it the best possible thriller. If you write a serious work of art, he will try to make it what it is meant to be, and not make you turn it into a thriller or a Harlequin romance. If you have ever worked as an editor or a sub-subeditor of a magazine, you know that all second-rate stories submitted tend to sound alike. Certain devices that the ordinary writer could not guess to be old hat—such as a compulsive use of the third-person-limited point of view, or the habit of starting every story with the weather ("It was unseasonably cool that morning," or "The sun hung directly overhead")—prove so commonplace that one feels compelled to avoid them in one's own fiction. Editors' experience makes them sensitive to these clichés, and one is wise to listen as objectively as possible. If it seems to the writer that the editor's comments on his novel are wrong, my advice is that he write back and defend himself. If the writer's defense is foolish or petty (if it reveals a personality much worse than the editor guessed from the novel), the editor is likely to drop the novelist. Who needs a crank pen pal? But if the writer is correct and states his case intelligently, the editor is likely to pay attention.

The first editor to look with a certain amount of interest at my work was Bob Gottlieb at Knopf. I went unpublished for a long time, as I've already mentioned, so I had a number of novels waiting for someone to notice them. When I sent *Grendel* to Gottlieb he was puzzled by it and wrote a letter full of reserved admiration and doubts. Being young and foolish, I assumed he was giving me the brush-off, so I sent the book elsewhere, to no avail. Later I sent him *The Sunlight Dialogues*, which he suggested that I cut by a third. I responded with a postcard: "Which third?" (He didn't answer.) A few months thereafter, the late David Segal, then at New American Library, read my work; he was partly influenced by William Gass, who had recommended me (and was then publishing, under Segal's editorship, *Omensetter's Luck*), and partly influenced by my arrival at his office in a black leather motorcycle jacket, carrying a shopping bag full of manuscripts—*The Resurrection*, *The Wreckage of Agathon*, and *Grendel*. (The rest of the story is embarrassing but I'll tell it anyway.) I placed on Segal's desk the three novels I'd biked into town with and said, "Mr. Segal, I'd like you to read these novels," and then, after a pause, "Now." David Segal was a kind man, though not really one to be bullied. He began to read, went through two or three pages, then said, "Mr. Gardner, I can't read your fiction while you're watching." So I left. When he arrived at his office the next morning at ten he told me he was taking all three novels. He published one at New American Library, then moved to Harper and published one there, then moved to Knopf, where he was in the process of publishing *Grendel* and *The Sunlight Dialogues*, which he'd subsequently accepted, when, to this world's great loss, he died.

David Segal's style was probably unusual in the publishing world. He accepted my books on the basis of the merit he saw in them and only then told me what he thought wrong. I have a long letter from him about *The Sunlight Dialogues* in which he tells me where the symbolism has gone amiss, where the language is excessive, and so on. (Though he did not say it, one implication of his letter was that I should cut the book by a third.) Because he approached me as he did, treated me as a serious novelist and attacked the work on its own grounds, I found it easy to listen. Later, after he died and I began to work with Bob Gottlieb, I came to understand that they both knew the same things; the difference was one of style. Bob Gottlieb hints at what's wrong, sometimes stating the problem meta-phorically. (The novelist Harry Crews once wrote a scathing *Esquire* piece mocking Bob Gottlieb for saying Crews should let his novel "breathe." Some who have read Crews's work would say Gottlieb was right.) Other editors work in other ways. Some write long, thorough letters after the first reading; some prefer to talk informally with the writer; some make almost no comment but take the book as it stands (these last are rare). All of them, though they may at times be off the mark, are serious, careful people.

Once the novel is accepted, the editor goes through the manuscript again and marks it up, suggesting cuts, improve-ments, expansions, reworkings. I have found that some editors edit with a light hand, while others question almost every line. Usually I'm happy with either kind of editing. On rare occa-sions one hits a stubborn, wrongheaded editor, and then one is in trouble. The editor of one of my novels (not Gottlieb or Segal) insisted on changing my punctuation, forcing it to con-form to some rule he learned at Yale and denying absolutely the notion that punctuation can be an art. One of the characters in the novel was unable to remember people's names and used any name that came into his head. The editor fixed all this. When I howled, he said nothing, and he refused to change anything back. I don't know what the writer is supposed to do in a case like this—probably withdraw the manuscript. Cer-tainly don't go to that editor again. That kind of experience is rare, or at least it has been rare for me. On the whole, editors are flexible and respect the author's wishes.

Now the manuscript goes through copy editing. The writer's literary editor turns the book over to another kind of editor, a maniac for details, who goes through the book check-ing spelling, accuracy of statement, consistency of style, and so on, and giving any necessary instructions to the typesetter. When the job is finished, the copy editor sends the marked-up manuscript back to the writer with pink slips of paper attached, giving the copy editor's queries. The writer takes or rejects each of the editor's corrections, and the manuscript goes to the typesetter. After a short while (a few weeks, in my experience), the writer gets the galleys—long pages from the typesetter, marked up by the proofreader for typographical errors. The writer rechecks what the copy editor has checked, notes mistakes, sends the galleys back, and waits for the book. Sometimes writers are still rewriting at the galley stage. Changes at this point cost money, and the writer who suddenly has a major new vision of his novel is sure to make his publisher unhappy. If the book is high art, or if it's one the publisher is sure will make a fortune, galley changes may not be a matter for concern. But ordinarily one should alter galleys sparingly.

After the book arrives in the writer's mailbox, and after it has finally reached the bookstores, the writer wrings his hands over a new problem: promotion. Writers are almost never satisfied with the promotion job their publishers do. There's nothing wrong with complaining and exerting any pressure one can to get more, bigger, and better ads, nothing wrong with getting the publicity department to try to arrange TV interviews and so on; but the writer should understand that the game is now pretty much out of his hands. Publishers generally know what kinds of books will benefit from aggressive promotion and what kinds of books, no matter how hard you push them, won't take off. Like other businesspeople, publishers invest where they expect their investment to pay. The masterful promotion job done on John Irving's *The World According to Garp* (jackets in various colors; large ads in major papers and magazines; for all I know, T-shirts and bumper stickers) obviously paid off; but the same campaign used on another novel, even an earlier novel by John Irving, might have been a waste of time and money. *Garp* is one of those novels that can be viewed either as a serious work of art or as a book for a mass audience, containing, as it does, the requisite sex, strange violence, and concern with great questions of the moment (e.g., feminism). If the book had not in fact had the kind of appeal its promoters claimed for it, the publisher's credibility would have dropped, readers and bookstore managers would have been angry, and John Irving would have done less well on his next novel. Since promotion departments are usually efficient, it is probably not very beneficial to yell and scream at them, or to insist on the publisher's writing into the contract the amount of money guaranteed for promotion. (If he gives the writer more money for promotion, he'll take it away elsewhere, for instance lopping off part of the advance. And if the publisher is right about how much promotion to use and where it will become a matter of diminishing returns, the writer who demands more promotion and accepts a lower advance to get it is robbing himself.) As for TV interviews and the like—things that cost the publisher nothing—the writer can choose to do as many as he pleases or can get. (He may get none, of course.) His publisher's promotion department can try to arrange, in various cities, book-and-author luncheons, or get the writer onto all-night radio talk shows. If the writer proves extraordinarily charming, such strategies may do wonders.

So much for the writer's relationship with his publisher. Let me turn to the writer's need for the support of those around him. However tough the peasant in his heart, every writer needs people who believe in him, give him a shoulder to cry on, and value what he values. If the writer doesn't get it, he might try changing friends. Above all, I think, it pays to seek out other writers—taking a writing class, going to readings if there are any he can get to, attending a summer writers' conference.

Summer conferences sometimes offer beginning writers a good chance to meet editors and agents, get their fiction evaluated by famous older writers and fast-rising younger writers, and meet other serious beginners suffering some of the same troubles they have, aesthetic, psychological, and social. The writing community encountered at such a conference does not end, for many people, when the conference ends. It is common for conferees to write to one another through the year, meet once or twice in some convenient city, and look for help, long after the conference, from conference instructors. One hears the complaint that conferences lead to a kind of writer incest: we find one instructor praising another's book on the book jacket, or reviewing it in *The New York Times*, and so forth. What is really involved is almost always a senior conference instructor giving help to the book of a younger instructor or a conference student. Friendships (not to mention love affairs) can be intense at conferences. No doubt this has to do with the frenetic atmosphere bred by the brevity of the conference—the student's hunger to learn everything he can, the teacher's responsiveness to it, and the occasional escapes into pressure-relieving revels. From every point of view, except in the instance of the bad writer who goes away feeling ignored by his teachers and fellow students—that is, goes off psychologically less strong than when he came—writers' conferences are wonderful ego boosters for young writers.

Professionally, the young novelist's most valuable support is his agent. Poets and writers of short stories don't need an agent as badly and probably can't get one anyway: there's ordinarily not enough money in poetry and short stories to make the agent's expenditure of time worthwhile. If the short story writer prints a few stories in high-paying magazines like *The New Yorker*, he may be able to attract an agent, but he obviously doesn't need one. He can sell his own stories, and with a magazine one can't use an agent to jack up the price. But for a young novelist, an agent is all but indispensable, even if, thanks to powerful friends or freaky good luck, he's able to sell his novel on his own. A good agent knows what the going rates are, knows editors personally and can accurately gauge how hard a given one can be pushed. The innocent writer can be eaten alive by a publisher's contract. It's common for publishers to try to take a share of movie rights, foreign rights, anything they can grab. Only an experienced agent knows when to make a canceling sweep of the pen.

Agents are also of value, of course, in getting the writer's work sold. Agents may not work as hard at selling as the writer would do himself. They have a stable of writers to work with, and no personal urgency; they know from experience that the good fiction that comes into their office will probably sooner or later be bought. Ordinarily they don't mind if the writer tries to sell things on his own (they get their ten percent anyway) and if the writer has the proper temperament he may want to do some of the selling, keeping the agent in reserve for contract negotiations. On the other hand, an agent can take pressure off a writer. Whereas after a certain number of rejections the writer is likely to give up on a story or novel, the agency goes on, impartial as a pulsar, sending out the fiction, getting it back, sending it out again. (Agents usually know better than writers do when to give up.) And whereas the writer is likely to be humbled or enraged by letters of rejection, with all their perhaps foolish advice about how to fix the book, agents tend to be unimpressed. At the writer's instruction, the agent will tell him nothing of what editors advise—except if some editor comes up with a suggestion that seems to the agent important. While writers may feel self-doubt—after twenty published books, I still often ask myself if I'm really a writer —and while editors have grievous responsibilities, the agent deals in simple yeses and noes, more dollars or less dollars. As long as he has reason to trust his own judgment (from repeatedly selling his clients' books), he expects editors to pay attention to his judgment, and the force of his conviction helps make it happen. An agent, in short, is a good person to have on your side.

Getting a good agent can be almost as hard as getting a publisher. One should avoid dealing with an agent who charges a reading fee. It's usually against the policy of the literary agents' associations and suggests that the agent may be in the business of fleecing amateur writers. (If one takes in enough reading fees, one never needs to sell a book.) For information on reliable agents, or to contact an agent, write to ILAA (Independent Literary Agents Association), Box 5257, FDR Station, New York, N.Y. 10150. This organization includes younger agents, the kind most likely to take on a new writer, if the writer does not have strong recommendations from someone famous. Or write Society of Authors' Representatives, P.O. Box 650, Old Chelsea Station, New York, N.Y. 10113. Tell the agency head in brief, clear terms what kind of writer you are and what kind of book you want to sell. (If the agency doesn't answer your letter, fine; that's one agency you don't want.) You need to write a smart letter, of course. If the letter contains bad writing (tiresome chattiness, jargon, crabbed syntax), the agent will know he doesn't want you. With agents as with anybody else, name dropping helps. If you've studied with famous writers, mention them. If you've published stories or won prizes, mention that.

In the normal course of things, one or more agencies will write back asking to see your work. Send it. (Neatness counts. Nobody, including agents, wants to labor through a manuscript that's barely legible.) If every agency in the end turns you down, you will know you're either not good enough or too good. If you're too good, keep writing, keep your contacts with the writing community available to you, and eventually your day will come.

One last word on this subject. Rejection by an agent means more, usually, than rejection by an editor. Agents seldom explain in detail why they've rejected a writer, but they have, invariably, only one reason: they do not think they can sell the writer's work. They may think it's wonderful, they may think it's awful; but they don't think they can peddle it. The only agent you want is the one who wants you. As I've said, it may help if a famous writer introduces you—certainly the young writer should tug the coattails of every famous writer he can get near without making him angry—but in the end, agents trust no one but themselves. That's why they prosper, and why their clients prosper.

While one is learning one's craft, then practicing it and hunting for an agent, then waiting for mail with the agent's return address, one must somehow make a living. Every writer hopes, like a medieval Christian, that after his period of honorable suffering, bliss will follow as a reward. So the writer takes some miserable part-time job, or lives off his parents or spouse, and writes and prays and waits. One day, the writer tells himself, the big break will come, and his money troubles will be over.

It's not true. At any rate, it's not true for the serious writer. Maybe one in a thousand serious novelists ever become self-supporting by means of their art. The writer, for all his childishness, needs to face this fact and deal with it.

Through the centuries writers have found various tricks for survival. Ancient poets begged or attached themselves to kings. There are still, here and there in the world, decent rich people who will give financial help to the promising writer, knowing they will probably never get paid back. The usual means by which the rich give help to the noble poor is through foundations—the Guggenheim, for instance. Or the writer may seek public support, from the National Endowment for the Arts or the arts councils in the various states. The extremely good writer has a chance with such organizations, especially if he knows well-known writers who can testify to his worth. But there is inevitably a certain amount of crookedness in foundations and grant programs. Somebody has to judge the writer's merit, and judges have friends whose work friendship causes to shine more brightly than it otherwise might. The writer without friends may be at a disadvantage. Or the judges on foundation boards may have some particular kind of fiction they like, so that even if they recognize an applicant as outstanding, they give their money to someone else. If the young writer can get some rich individual to back him, he should swallow his pride and do it. For organizations that can help the young novelist, locate good teachers, get advice on fellowships, and so on, write or phone Poets & Writers, 201 West 54th Street, New York, N.Y. 10019 (phone [212] 757-1766). The magazine published by Poets & Writers, *Coda* (annual subscription rate, $10), has complete, up-to-date information on contests, fellowships, and money available to writers through arts councils and foundations.

More likely, the writer will have to find a job. Almost all full-time jobs are hard on writing, even office work where one has practically nothing to do. I myself cannot write with people around me—I need solitude both for concentration and for the freedom to go through without embarrassment the kind of gesturing, wincing, and mumbling I often need to get a scene right. Also, I cannot work on a novel if I do not have long time blocks for writing—fifteen hours straight is for me ideal. Trying to nickel and dime your way through a five-hundred-page novel can drive you crazy. Some writers, in hopes of solving such problems, take work as fire watchers and sit alone in high lookout posts, occasionally glancing at the horizon. Theoretically that ought to be an ideal situation, but in practice it's a pain, mainly because the CB never quits. Jobs as night watchman or night hotel clerk are not much better, and trying to earn a living by teaching high school is much worse—nothing is more draining, even for a teacher not overburdened by a sense of responsibility. Journalism may be a better option, but it may undermine the writer's prose and sensibility.

One of the favorite jobs of writers in recent years has been college teaching. College teachers get the summer off and even in winter are likely to find more time for writing than almost anybody else except the full-time hobo. One teaches, say, three classes, each three hours a week, sees students for several hours each week (with luck, one can bunch up appointments so they all come on Tuesday or Wednesday), spends a few hours preparing classes (if one is unusually conscientious), and the rest of the time is his own. For the writer of suitable temperament, university teaching may be an excellent solution. The trouble is that there are fewer and fewer jobs. MFA and PhD programs turn out far more writers looking to teach than the market can absorb. That fact perhaps need not be utterly discouraging. The extraordinary student is still employable. His strong recommendations from professors and his fine record of publications, whether in fiction or in his chosen academic field, may pry open doors that to others seem rusted shut. And for another, a PhD in any respectable field—English literature, for instance, or even philosophy—helps to crack doors elsewhere, for instance in government, advertising, or business.

The writer who survives by teaching writing may discover, however, that his teaching hurts his art. Dealing day in and day out with beginning writers, he finds himself forced continually to think in analytical fashion about problems he would normally solve in other ways. To make his student see clearly what is wrong in his or her fiction, the writer-teacher has no choice but to work in a fully conscious, intellectual way. Every writer at some point must go through an analytical period, but in time he must get his own characteristic solutions into his blood, so that when confronted by a problem in a novel he's writing he does not consult his literary background. He *feels* his way to the solution; rather than drawing back from the fictional dream to look at what he's doing, he solves the problem by plunging deeper into the dream. For the writing teacher, the habit of intellectual analysis may become crippling.

He may encounter other problems. As the teacher sees more and more talented students, he may consciously or unconsciously begin to set himself increasingly difficult tasks, distancing himself from his best students' work by tour-de-force showmanship, pyrotechnics, and subtlety beyond his students' means. He becomes precious, arty, academic. And because it is necessary for a teacher to awaken his students to the various possibilities of contemporary fiction, so they don't all write alike, as if Donald Barthelme were the only writer who ever lived (or Hemingway or Salinger or whoever is most influential in a given class), the teacher may become unduly influenced by other writers of his time, or unduly concerned with theory. No doubt, for some teachers of writing this never happens; but one hears it as a common complaint.

However he goes about it, what the writer must do, assuming he's not independently wealthy, is to find some kind of congenial work that will not eat up all his energy and time. For example, delivering rural route mail is terrific (one can get off by noon). And for the sake of his art he must learn to live within the limits his odd existence sets. If the writer wants everything he sees on TV, he'd better quit writing and get serious about money or else give away his TV to the poor in spirit.

The most obvious escape from the debilitating effects of one's competitive, ware-hawking culture is to move out of it —go to Mexico or Portugal or Crete. This is exactly what many writers do, but the cost of living cheaply may be greater than one at first imagined. Also, by leaving one's culture one may lose one's material. Expatriation may be all right for the fabulist, the nonrealistic writer. But again and again through history, writers have found that in leaving the people they know best—the specific kind of culture they come from—they leave the wellspring of their art. So the English novelist Arnold Bennett, when he left his country origins for London's brighter lights, found himself a weakened writer. Such examples might be multiplied. Some writers thrive on transplanting, of course. Leslie Fiedler claims that Missoula, Montana, was the very best place for him to live for twenty years because all the differences between Missoula and New York stimulated his imagination; also, the nights were long and there wasn't much for him to do except write. The shock of an unfamiliar culture was equally beneficial to Malcolm Lowry, Graham Greene, and Henry James, not to mention Dante. But the risk is there; one should be ready for it. Many writers feel they suffer from being set down in a region—usually because of a teaching job —so different from their appropriate milieu (New Englanders in Southern California, Texans in Cleveland) that they feel diminished, unreal to themselves. A special case of this general problem is the transplanting of the lower-class writer to some setting, especially the university, where gentrification undermines his language and values or otherwise denatures his experience of the world.

The best way a writer can find to keep himself going is to live off his (or her) spouse. The trouble is that, psychologically at least, it's hard. Even if one's spouse is rich, it's hard. Our culture teaches none of its false lessons more carefully than it teaches that one should never be dependent. Hence the novice or still unsuccessful writer, who has enough trouble believing in himself, has the added burden of shame. That's one reason writers, like other artists, have so often chosen to live off people that, at some conscious or unconscious level, they need not respect—generous prostitutes, say. It's hard to be a good writer and a guilty person; a lack of self-respect creeps into one's prose. Yet for all that may be said against it, living off one's spouse or lover is an excellent survival tactic. For some businessmen, nothing gives more satisfaction than a wife or lover's artistic achievement; and some women, in a way that only a cynic would call morbid, derive pride and satisfaction from enabling an artist husband or lover to do his work. I do not mean that the writer should seek out someone on whom he can feed like a vampire. But if a writer finds himself living, for honest reasons, with someone glad to support his art, he or she should make every effort to shake off the conventional morality and accept God's bounty, doing everything in his power to make the lover's generosity worthwhile.

With luck, the writer may eventually make money. A novel may be taken by the movies, or by the Book-of-the-Month Club, or may for some reason win the hearts of the young. But one ought not to count on it. Most novelists, including very good ones, never make a living from their art. The average income of professional writers is, I think, something like five or six thousand dollars a year. A young novelist can hardly help hoping that someday he will be published and will find himself free of guilt and debt, but—statistically, at least—shattered expectations are part of the game. One study showed that about seventy percent of those who published a first novel in a given year never went on to publish another. If one is unwilling to write like a true artist, mainly because one needs to, one might do well to put one's energies somewhere else.

IV.

FAITH

In my experience, the single question most often asked during question-and-answer periods in university auditoriums and classrooms is: "Do you write with a pen, a typewriter, or what?" I suspect the question is more important than it seems on the surface. It brings up magical considerations—the kinds of things compulsive gamblers are said to worry about: When one plays roulette, should one wear a hat or not, and if one should, should one cock it to the left or to the right? What color hat is luckiest? The question about writing equipment also implies questions about that ancient daemon Writer's Block, about vision and revision, and, at its deepest level, asks whether or not there is really, for the young writer, any hope.

1

As every writer knows—both the experienced and the inexperienced—there is something mysterious about the writer's ability, on any given day, to write. When the juices are flowing, or the writer is "hot," an invisible wall seems to fall away, and the writer moves easily and surely from one kind of reality into another. In his noninspired state, the writer feels all the world to be mechanical, made up of numbered separate parts: he does not see wholes but particulars, not spirit but matter; or to put it another way, in this state the writer keeps looking at the words he's written on the page and seeing only words on a page, not the living dream they're meant to trigger. In the writing state—the state of inspiration—the fictive dream springs up fully alive: the writer forgets the words he has written on the page and sees, instead, his characters moving around their rooms, hunting through cupboards, glancing irritably through their mail, setting mousetraps, loading pistols. The dream is as alive and compelling as one's dreams at night, and when the writer writes down on paper what he has imagined, the words, however inadequate, do not distract his mind from the fictive dream but provide him with a fix on it, so that when the dream flags he can reread what he's written and find the dream starting up again. *This and nothing else is the desperately sought and tragically fragile writer's process: in his imagination, he sees made-up people doing things—sees them clearly—and in the act of wondering what they will do next he sees what they will do next, and all this he writes down in the best, most accurate words he can find, understanding even as he writes that he may have to find better words later, and that a change in the words may mean a sharpening or deepening of the vision, the fictive dream or vision becoming more and more lucid, until reality, by comparison, seems cold, tedious, and dead.* This is the process he must learn to set off at will and to guard against hostile mental forces.

Every writer has experienced at least moments of this strange, magical state. Reading student fiction one can spot at once where the power turns on and where it turns off, where the writer wrote from "inspiration," or deep, flowing vision, and where he had to struggle along on mere intellect. One can write whole novels without once tapping the mysterious center of things, the secret room where dreams prowl. One can easily make up characters, plot, setting, and then fill in the book like a paint-by-numbers picture. But most stories and novels have at least moments of the real thing, some exactly right gesture or startlingly apt metaphor, some brief passage describing wallpaper or the movement of a cat, a passage that some-how shines or throbs as nothing around it does, some fictional moment that, as we say, "comes alive." It is this experience of seeing something one has written come alive—literally, not metaphorically, a character or scene daemonically entering the world by its own strange power, so that the writer feels not the creator but only the instrument, or conjurer, the priest who stumbled onto the magic spell—it is this experience of tapping some magic source that makes the writer an addict, willing to give up almost anything for his art, and makes him, if he fails, such a miserable human being.

The poison or miraculous ointment—it can be either one or both—comes at first in small doses. The usual experience of young writers is that during the process of writing the first draft they feel that all they write is alive, full of interest, but then when they look at the writing the next day they find most of it dull and lifeless. Then comes one small moment qualita-tively different from the rest: one small dose of the real thing. The more numerous those moments, the more powerful the resulting addiction. The magic moment, notice, has nothing to do with *theme* or, in the usual sense, *symbolism*. It has nothing to do, in fact, with the normal subject matter of literature courses. It is simply a psychological hot spot, a pulsation on an otherwise dead planet, a "real toad in an imaginary garden." These queer moments, sometimes thrilling, sometimes just strange, moments setting off an altered state, a brief sense of escape from ordinary time and space—moments no doubt sim-ilar to those sought by religious mystics, or those experienced by people near death—are the soul of art, the reason people pursue it. And young writers sufficiently worried about achieving this state to know when they've done it and feel dissatisfied when they haven't are already on the way to calling it up at will, though they may never come to understand how they do it. The more often one finds the magic key, whatever it is, the more easily the soul's groping fingers come to land on it. In magic as in other things, success brings success.

But it is not all magic. Once one knows by experience the "feel" of the state one is after, there are things one can do to encourage its onset. (Some writers, with practice, become able to drop into the creative state at any moment; others have difficulty all their lives.) Every writer must figure out for himself, if he can, how he personally works best.

Let us go back to the matter of the pen, pencil, or typewriter. There is of course no right answer to the question: "Should one write with a pen or a typewriter or what?" nor is the question worth answering except insofar as it reveals something about the creative process. Think for a moment about the very young writer, the writer of high-school or early college age. Not yet a good typist, he sits staring at the paper in his typewriter, distracted by the look of the type on the page, distracted by the fact that the paper's not quite centered, distracted by the unmanageability of the keys and, if the typewriter's electric, the impatient, henpecking hum. The writer knows that if he can ever get good at typing, writing on a typewriter will be faster, but in the meantime he seems unable to write at all. At last he tears the paper out of the typewriter, crumples it in his fist, and throws it in the wastebasket, then starts over with a pen. He begins to get into the scene he means to write—he begins to see people moving around as they're supposed to do, getting themselves into trouble as his idea for the story requires—and then, as the writer glances over what he's written, trying to get a "run" on the place where he has gotten stuck, he notices that the ink is smudged. He tries to ignore it, throwing himself back into the fictive dream, but that smudge keeps nagging. At last he copies over what he's written onto clean paper, then once more reads from the top, trying to throw himself into the dream so that when he comes to the point where his imagination failed, the dream will keep going of its own momentum, he'll "see" what the characters must do next.

The trouble, he discovers, is that handwriting, like speech, is full of gestures. We don't normally think about that fact, unless we're amateur analysts of handwriting. Nevertheless it's the case: just as when we're speaking we give conscious or unconscious signals of our feelings, accidentally curling the lip or glancing away evasively, so, too, our writing gives off second-by-second signals of our happiness or uncertainty or weariness or secret dishonesty and bluff. We do not necessarily know all this as we look over what we've written, but we find ourselves noticing the penmanship; it begins to stand like a stone wall between us and the fictive dream. We do not see a dog rummaging through garbage cans but, instead, individual words: A   dog   was.

I don't know whether any very young writer besides myself ever really suffered the woes I've been assigning him (perhaps not, except for the part about the typewriter: I had a terrible time learning to write on one, and I know many writers who've never managed it); but what I'm saying about the distracting quality of mechanics is meant to illuminate by analogy a darker problem, the distracting quality of words. Even for the expert writer, and much more noticeably for the relative beginner, language is, like an unfamiliar typewriter, a complicated, overawing, clumsy, and impatiently nagging machine. You stare at the fictive dream, you try to get it down in words, and you find language resisting you. You want to say: "She intended to tell him so-and-so"; you decide she should *go* to him and tell him, so you shift to: "She intended on going to him and . . ." but one can't say "intended on"; and you're pulled out of the dream. It's a trifle, this recalcitrance of language (especially in the example I've given, since the problem is too easily solved), but the nuisance is real. Most of the young novelists I've worked with had problems initially with idiomatic English. Which is correct for an authorial, non-dialectal voice: "She thought that she should tell him" or "She thought she should tell him"? Is it correct to say: "She'd anticipated that he would be angry"? (Should one say: "She'd anticipated his anger"?) Most writers for some reason come from the middle or lower middle class, at least in America, and very few lack quirks of speech that betray their origins; such oddities as, for instance, the New York City middle-class substitution of "bring" for "take," or "came" for "went," or the idiom "stood on line" for, as the rest of the country says, "stood in line." As long as one clings to the safest approaches (first-person narration, or third-person-limited), linguistic quirks may be texturally enriching; but as soon as the writer tries something more august—omniscient narration, or first-person narration by Bismarck or the Virgin Mary—the quirks make the writer look ignorant. Fiction in dialect has its interest, and as writers like Faulkner prove, it is possible to write large, deep-breathing fictions without unlearning one's dialect. (Instead of the usual king's English spoken by most omniscient authors, Faulkner uses a distinct Southern voice, one that does not distinguish between "infer" and "imply.") But whatever the beauties of dialect, few writers possessed of the ambition that characterizes the novelist want to be barred forever from the high tone of a Mann or Proust or Melville. So there stands language, difficult and intimidating, throwing roadblocks in the way of the writer's attempt to get the fictive dream onto the page.

And as smudges on the page written in ink, or gestural signs in the writer's handwriting, distract our hypothetical young writer from what it is he is trying to say, so blurs and the uncontrolled secondary meanings of words distract and impede. If a character in a story tells us that some thoroughly incompetent, feeble king now being carried to his grave "was born dead," meaning that the king was never really alive at all, the word "born" puns on "borne" (carried), and—unless we understand that the speaker means to be witty—we are distracted. Every writer can give examples from his own experience of how language slips and slides, turning serious moments cheap, making the writer look silly ("a two-headed lady's snake ring"), obfuscating meaning, or slyly turning the writer into a hypocrite or pretentious fool. So the writer copies down his fictive dream, then looks at the words he chose with such care and blushes like one willfully misunderstood, betrayed. Or the words say exactly what he meant, but so carefully that they make him seem prissy and self-conscious.

The trouble is not that the writer can't start up the fictive dream in his mind. If that were the trouble he wouldn't have written any words at all. The trouble is that having started up the dream and written some of it down, he's become suddenly self-conscious, self-doubting. The dreaming part is angel-like: it is the writer's eternal, childlike spirit, the daydreaming being who exists (or seems to) outside time. But the part of the writer that handles the mechanics, typing or writing with pencil or pen, choosing one word instead of another, is human, fallible, vulnerable to anxiety and shame. Making mistake after mistake, the beast in the writer begins to sweat and grind its teeth, longing to be raised up once more by the redeeming angel within—but miserably unworthy, shy in the presence of the holy, and afraid of heights.

So far, all I've said treats language as a recalcitrant and passive medium, the indifferent clay to be shaped into a figure, or the lead on which the image is to be stamped. Actually, language plays a far more active role in the creative process. No doubt it is sometimes true that the writer has an intuition of what it is he wants to say and, after a struggle, finds just the right words to express the meaning he knew was there waiting to be expressed. Just as often—probably more often—language actively drives the writer to meanings he had no idea he would come to. This process is easier to show in poetry than in prose, though I'll try to show it in both. Let me start with a poem of my own, not because I claim skill as a poet but because it seems to me an adequate poem of its kind and, more important, I know exactly the process by which it took the shape it has.

> Lovely, spooky, dark blue Gentian,
> Inner walls like speckled snakeskin,
> Trumpet shaped, fit for a small
> Angel's grimly puckered lips
> Set on the Last Day to call
> Ants and bees to Apocalypse,
> What sins too minute to mention
> Wouldst thou bring to man's attention,
> Lovely, spooky, dark blue Gentian?

I will not dwell on my various false starts in trying to get this poem down but will simply explain the choices I finally made. Having a heavy teaching load and numerous nonfictional writing responsibilities (including this book), and having therefore no time to write fiction, I decided to write a poem, a flower poem since I thought I might someday publish a book of children's flower poems to match an earlier children's book of mine on animals. I found a picture of the dark blue gentian and looked at it to see what one might say. The main things I could think of to say, at least in the light of this particular photograph, were that the flower was pretty and that it looked ominous, the luminous dark blue of nightmare. My mind stumbled around in search of a suitably gloomy rhythm and possible words to fit with it and so came up with the first line. Obviously the gloom is slightly tongue-in-cheek (flowers usually aren't good candidates for the truly scary), hence the word choice "lovely," a word one can never take quite as seriously as it would like to be taken, and "spooky," a kid's word that, in a thudding trochaic rhythm, gets drawn out a little, inflated as it would be in a ghost story told orally to kids at camp. It's this same tongue-in-cheek seriousness that made me decide to capitalize "Gentian," giving it a faintly old-timey, Romantic quality (the Romantics were nothing if not naively earnest, as some of them, like Blake, at times understood).

Once the first line was down, I looked back at the picture for a clue to the second line (What else can I say?), knowing this line could rhyme or not, though rhythmic possibilities were limited slightly (the line must satisfy the ear as consonant with the line already in existence); and I saw immediately the odd fact reported in the second line, that the throat of the flower has a speckled, waxy sheen like snakeskin—and noticed in the same instant that "snakeskin" rhymes with "gentian," or anyway comes close enough for government work. After a little muddling in search of solemn trochees meaning "throat," I came upon "inner walls" and the line fell into place. Looking back at the picture for what more I might say, I noticed the most obvious thing about the flower, that it's trumpet-shaped, and wrote that down. Where to go from there? Perhaps some-one suitably ominous (in keeping with the choices I'd made so far) might be imagined as playing the trumpet. (If I'd said "bell shaped," another legitimate trochee, the idea of a small instru-mentalist would probably not have come up.) My childhood interest in—and slight uneasiness about—religion came to my rescue, as it so often does in my writing, and I thought of the Doomsday angel. Since after many years of practice I've learned—so that I no longer have to stop and think about it—that every character who enters a fiction needs vivid rendering, I chose words that would make my angel individual ("grimly puckered lips"; this angel of doom is personally *involved* in his work, no mere functionary); and now the natural requirements of drama raised the next question: If the angel is so concerned, whom or what is he behaving so sternly toward—elves? small children? The answer simply came to me; that is, I saw it in the fictive dream: bugs of some kind (natural inhabitants of the garden's small world, and enemies of flowers). I chose ants and bees partly because those creatures have, for me, a certain inherent nastiness, and partly because the word "ants" has a hard, nasty sound, as does "bees," to a lesser extent, but the effect is nonetheless there, especially if you push the z sound. I now had a mock-solemn set of lines in an old, easily recogniz-able literary tradition, the Moralizing Verse. What solemn lesson could I squeeze out of my setup? It occurred to me that the question was absurd, that maybe the whole Moralizing Verse tradition was at least just a little absurd, a way of bullying the young, so that what was needed was a comically sententious close—chiming rhymes, the mock formality and churchiness of "Wouldst thou bring," and the preacherly rhetoric of the last line's echoing of the poem's first line—a device that especially pleased me because, in the orthodox view, Doomsday brings Christian history full circle.

Lest my main point here be lost in my argument's details, let me reiterate it: words not only serve but help to shape the fictive vision. I had no inkling, when I started the poem, that I would write about a tiny angel or Doomsday as it applies to ants and bees, or, ultimately, the way grownups bully children with fables.

Poems "write themselves" more visibly than short stories or novels do, since it's a little difficult, though by no means impossible, to write a short story without some idea of the plot, and extremely difficult to write a novel without a carefully constructed, though tentative, plan. But the process I've been describing in relation to poetry does operate, and not just occasionally, in one's writing of a novel. The following passage occurs near the end of one of my novels, *October Light*.

> The two ancient creatures stared at one another, both of them standing more or less upright—the bear considerably more upright than the man—the old man unable to do a thing to defend himself, too weak-kneed to try running or even jump for the gun, his heart so hammering at the root of his throat that he could not even make a sound. He often thought, going over it later, how that Britisher must have felt when he looked up at the top of the wall by the cliff, there at Fort Ticonderoga, and beheld that stone man Ethan Allen towering against the stars and gray dawn, filling the sky with his obscenities. He, the Britisher, had been an ordinary man, as James Page, here among his hives, was only an ordinary man. Ethan Allen had been put upon the earth, like

Hercules, to show an impression of things beyond it. So it was with this enormous old bear that stood sniffing at the wind and studying him, uncertain what heaven had in mind. A full minute passed, and still the bear stood considering, as if baffled by where the old man had come from and what his purpose could be, creeping up on him. Then at last the bear went down on all fours again, turned to where the containers for the honeycombs sat, and began—as if he had all day and had forgotten James' existence—to eat. James made for the gun and, despite the weakness of his legs, reached it. The bear turned, a low growl coming from low in his throat, then went back calmly to his business. James with wildly trembling hands raised the gun to his shoulder and aimed it at the back of the bear's head. What happened then he could not clearly remember afterward. As he was about to pull the trigger, something jerked the gun straight up—possibly, of course, his own arm. He fired at the sky, as if warning a burglar. The bear jumped three feet into the air and began shaking exactly as the old man was doing, snatched up an armload of honeycombs, and began to back off.

My analysis of the process behind this passage must of necessity be sketchy and brief. Given my tortuous way of working, revising and revising, such a passage, short as it is, may take weeks. A couple of points of background information: Throughout the novel, old man Page has more or less unconsciously associated bears with the otherworldly—with death and the possibility of divine retribution, forces no man can match; though, short of that final conflict, he has believed, stern courage like that of his earthly hero Ethan Allen can get a man through. Most of his life, James Page believed himself such a hero, but he has recently learned that his own stubborn meanness, his misapprehension of the heroic, lies behind his son's suicide and much other grief. The point of view controlling the passage is more or less omniscient, the narration moving in and out of James Page's consciousness.

Much here is simply a recording of the fictive dream (the stooped bear and man, the gun leaning against a hive, out of reach, the old bear's puzzled gaze), but language colors and helps determine events throughout. Calling the bear and man "ancient creatures" commits me to implications different from those involved in "old man and old bear": to me, a frequent teacher of courses in the epic, "ancient" summons up ancient Greece (hence in a moment Hercules will show up, bringing with him a central idea in Homer, that the gods conceive an ideal for man, an ideal revealed in the human world by the actions of a model hero like Achilles and transmitted to future generations by the epic poet, or the muses, or memory, or "epic song"); and "creatures" in its root sense (things God created) commits me to a set of ideas faintly in conflict with the first, a vision of both the old man and the seemingly mystical bear as mortal, tragically vulnerable, ultimately a view of all human heroism as illusion (hence the popular Vermont legends of Ethan Allen, almost none of them based on fact, will enter James's consciousness, specifically the legend that, dead drunk, leading a band of Indians, Ethan Allen climbed the unscalable cliff behind Ticonderoga and took the British guard by surprise). My comments on the relative uprightness of bear and man and the man's sense of helplessness come partly from a need to make the scene vivid and specific, partly from linguistic considerations. To express the tension of the situation, especially James Page's sense of panic, I need a long, rushing sentence: the rhythm appropriate to the mood helps call up phrases (looking at the picture in my mind, what can I say that will keep the sentence pounding?). Landing on the word "upright"—knowing the old man's feeling of inferiority (physical and spiritual) to the bear as he mystically understands it—I find it shades toward "righteous," as in "upright conduct," and his helplessness takes on overtones: Who can defend himself before the final judge? His sense of impotence calls up in my mind (because I'm a medievalist) the once common image of heaven as a castle or fort, which instantly becomes Fort Ticonderoga, high in its stone cliff, and, seemingly from nowhere, comes the image of that "stone man" Ethan Allen, "towering." From close recording of the fictive dream comes "the stars and gray dawn," but from deeper in the novel comes the image that follows. Throughout the novel the vivid light of October skies has been associated with the clarity and sense of doom in the mind of a man near the end of his life's season. Old man Page has been confident of his opinions, but now, understanding his guilt, knowing himself an "ordinary man," as he says, not a hero, much less a god, his mental sky is not noble though doomed, but obscene, polluted: insofar as the sky is heroic or divine, it curses him. (Partly the image comes from history, of course. Ethan Allen, gang leader and barn burner, was not a man of careful phrases.) Now, closely watching the bear, Page becomes increasingly conscious of its creature nature. If it's a Hercules—an epic model of heaven's will—it no longer remembers what message it was to bring; and, like a mortal creature encountering the unearthly, it cannot figure out where James Page came from. In the lines that follow, the bear becomes more and more a thing of nature, such a creature as James Page is.

Let me make clear, in case it's not, that I am not suggesting, by this analysis of how the passage came into being, that these subtleties of language and idea transformation are things the shrewd critic should or could point out. Many of them are private—for instance, my rapid association of Fort Ticonderoga with "stone man"—and others, like the allusion to Hercules and Homer's idea of the epic model, are of trifling significance in terms of the novel's larger meaning. I am describing only the way in which one choice of words leads to another, the way language actively influences the progress of events. When a writer finds himself stuck, it is not only because he cannot get down the fictive dream, that is, find the right words for it, but also because he's unable to go with the linguistic flow, unable to adapt what he wants to say to what his words are suggesting that he *might* say. He's like a sculptor so intent on the image in his mind that he's unwilling to compromise with—take suggestions from—the grain of the marble.

What is the writer to do? I think the answer is, given the writer's linguistic competence: *Have faith.* First, recognize that the art of writing is immensely more difficult than the beginning writer may at first believe but in the end can be mastered by anyone willing to do the work. Good writing involves the operation of many mental processes at once, and in the beginning one must deal with those many processes one at a time, breaking down the total job into its smallest segments: getting down roughly what one is trying to say; closely analyzing the words with which one has said it to see what they are saying (or refusing to say); then thinking about (*a*) how one can make the words stop saying what one does not want them to say and (*b*) how whatever it is that the words are saying might be turned to account. Second, trust that what works for other human activities will work for the activity of writing. Learning to ride a bicycle, one must learn to steer, learn to keep one's balance, learn to push the pedals, learn to stop without falling—all separate processes requiring separate focuses of concentration. Eventually they become one process.

Where does the writer get faith? Partly, as we've seen, from community support. The steady encouragement of friends makes it easier to slip into the dream and easier to endure the drudgery of learning both to control and to listen to language. And partly from the writer's selfless love of his art—a pleasure in writing, whether by other people or by himself, that makes him forget for the moment his limitations. This is why it is often helpful, when one cannot write, to read the fiction of some favorite writer. The older writer's dream world and dance of language come bursting into the mind, and one's own capacity for dreaming and playing with words comes unstuck. One starts writing, and if the dream is strong enough, and the words cooperative enough, the first-draft mistakes distract only as a fly in the corner of the room distracts, present and annoying but not overpowering as long as the writer is deeply involved in what he's doing and convinced that the result will probably justify the labor.

Since the problem of the writer unable to concentrate on the fictive dream or respond flexibly to the impulses of language is essentially a problem of inhibition, or the mind defeating itself, all of the conventional forms of breaking inhibition can be employed to get things rolling—self-hypnosis, TM, drunkenness and smoking, or falling in love. None of them are effective in the absence of hard work and occasional successes.

Let me pause to say a word here about autohypnosis, since I myself have at times found it effective (unless I'm fooling myself, which I may well be). A simple method is to sit in a chair with comfortable arms—preferably in a fairly dark, quiet room—your arms flat on the arms of the chair, and tell yourself with firm conviction (it will prove justified) that although you will not move a muscle, your hand and forearm are going to rise. Concentrate on not moving the arm, but without resisting whatever may begin to happen to the arm, and concentrate, too, on the belief that the arm will rise. You will soon begin to feel an odd lightness in the hand, and eventually, independent of conscious volition, the arm will lift. Magic. (A hypnotically raised arm can hang suspended in air for hours without discomfort. A hand raised by conscious will tires in minutes.) In this light hypnotic trance, make to yourself positive (never negative) suggestions: Tonight I will write with ease; or, tonight I'll feel no need to smoke so much. Most people discover that autohypnosis helps. Deep hypnosis by someone else, or more sophisticated forms of autohypnosis, may bring still greater benefit. If the trick doesn't work, never mind; sitting for half an hour in a dimly lit, quiet room is good for the psyche.

2

In its extreme form, the inhibition I've been describing ends in writer's block, not so much a failure of faith as a failure of will. The writer suffering writer's block can think of good plots and characters, or anyway he can think of good starts, which is all a healthy writer needs, but he can't persuade himself that they're worth writing down or developing. It's all been done before, he tells himself. And if he does, by a supreme effort, get down a few sentences, he finds the sentences disgustingly bad. In effect, a Platonic dream of what fiction ought to be has thrown its dark shadow not only over the actual rough draft the writer has begun, poisoning the writer's eye and robbing him of the strength it takes to transform the crude rough draft into a polished work of art, but over the very possibility of creating art.

Part of the writer's problem may be the wrong kind of appreciation: when he does work he knows to be less than he's capable of, his friends praise precisely those things he knows to be weak or meretricious. The writer who cannot write because nothing he writes is good enough, by his own standards, and because no one around him seems to share his standards, is in a special sort of bind: the love of good fiction that got him started in the first place makes him scornful of the flawed writing he does (nearly all first-draft writing is flawed), and his sense that nobody cares about truly good fiction robs him of motivation. This dissatisfaction is one the unusually talented writer may be especially prone to. Driven by the imperative "Make it new," he finds nothing he's written sufficiently original. In effect, he has failed to notice that originality is normally a quality achieved by diligence, not a natural condition. A glance at Hawthorne's first novel, *Fanshaw*, or any early piece by Melville, may prove instructive.

Another writer's blockage—a more serious blockage—may

arise from an excessive need for a success not actually related to good writing: an excessive need to please admirers (that is, to be loved), or prove himself vastly superior to others (that is, to be superhuman), or justify his existence against the too obstreperous cry of some old psychological wound (that is, to be redeemed). No amount of work can solve this writer's problem, because nothing he writes satisfies the actual motive behind it.

It is probably true that in some cases writer's block is incurable; but no useful purpose is served by making a great point of this, since one can never be sure whether a particular case will respond to treatment. As with all writer problems, it is usually a good idea for the writer to get as clear a notion as possible of just what is going wrong psychologically—whether on his own or with the help of someone trained in such things —and for the writer to understand that his problem, though perhaps uncommon, is not unheard of. In a given case, one or more of the following general observations may be helpful.

The writer should remind himself of how his writing went when he first began: tortuous labor and revision and gradual improvement, and first drafts at least as bad as the one he faces now—except that in those days he saw the faults less clearly, felt more excited by the possibilities, and was tricked by the exhilaration of new love. After the initial difficulties, the period of apprenticeship, writers have a tendency to think things ought to get easier. That rarely happens. As one learns more and more technical tricks, one finds oneself taking on more and more difficult projects. Instead of getting easier, one feels the work getting harder; or at any rate that's my experience. The writer impatient with his story idea, and impatient with whatever writing he can get down, has forgotten how fiction actually gets written.

Fiction, like sculpture or painting, begins with a rough sketch. One gets down the characters and their behavior any way one can, knowing the sentences will have to be revised, knowing the characters' actions may change. It makes no difference how clumsy the sketch is—sketches are not supposed to be polished and elegant. All that matters is that, going over and over the sketch as if one had all eternity for finishing one's story, one improves now this sentence, now that, noticing what changes the new sentences urge, and in the process one gets the characters and their behavior clearer in one's head, gradually discovering deeper and deeper implications of the characters' problems and hopes. Fiction does not spring into the world full grown, like Athena. It is the process of writing and rewriting that makes a fiction original and profound. One cannot judge in advance whether or not the idea of the story is worthwhile because until one has finished writing the story one does not know for sure what the idea *is;* and one cannot judge the style of a story on the basis of a first draft, because in a first draft the style of the finished story does not yet exist.

Sometimes when one cannot stand the story or novel one is working on, it helps to write something else—a different story or novel, or essays venting one's favorite peeves, or exercises aimed at passing the time and incidentally polishing up one's craft. The best way in the world for breaking a writer's block is to write a lot. Jabbering away on paper, one gets tricked into feeling interested, all at once, in something one is saying, and behold, the magic waters are flowing again. Often it helps to work on a journal, since that allows the writer to write about those things that most interest him, yet frees him of the pressure of achievement and encourages him to develop a more natural, more personal style. Almost any diversion from the overawing main job will do. I myself have kept going for years mainly by avoiding the one serious novel I mean to write someday. There it sits, five hundred rough-draft pages of it, watching me from its shelf like a skull. Nothing else I do is significant, by comparison, at least in my own mind. I am free to scatter words as an October wind scatters leaves.

Insofar as one's block comes mainly from outside oneself—

from a lack of useful appreciation, from social pressures of one kind or another, or from harsh criticism one feels to be just— there is little one can do except change one's life. The feeling that one's friends have no taste, even if it's true, is not a healthy feeling for a writer: it fills him with arrogance and self-pity, makes him a bad friend and, as a result, makes him a person plagued by secret guilt. One approach is to find a better pack of friends; another is to strive to become a more generous person. The latter way, if the writer can bring it off, will considerably enhance his odds of becoming a good writer if he ever starts working again. Occasionally, mean-spirited people have written good books, but the odds for it are long.

The best way of all for dealing with writer's block is never to get it. Some writers never do. Theoretically there's no reason one should get it, if one understands that writing, after all, is only writing, neither something one ought to feel deeply guilty about nor something one ought to be inordinately proud of. If children can build sand castles without getting sand-castle block, and if ministers can pray over the sick without getting holiness block, the writer who enjoys his work and takes measured pride in it should never be troubled by writer's block. But alas, nothing's simple. The very qualities that make one a writer in the first place contribute to block: hypersensitivity, stubbornness, insatiability, and so on. Given the general oddity of writers, no wonder there are no sure cures.

Writer's block comes from the feeling that one is doing the wrong thing or doing the right thing badly. Fiction written for the wrong reason may fail to satisfy the motive behind it and thus may block the writer, as I've said; but there is no wrong motive for writing fiction. At least in some instances, good fiction has come from the writer's wish to be loved, his wish to take revenge, his wish to work out his psychological woes, his wish for money, and so on. No motive is too low for art; finally it's the art, not the motive, that we judge.

As for writing in the wrong way, there is almost no wrong

way to write fiction; there are only ways that, for a given writer, are more efficient or less. Some respectable writers simply pour out onto paper everything that comes into their heads, then sift, edit, rearrange, and rewrite until a story of some kind emerges; others plan carefully and stick to the plan as closely as possible, so long as the characters don't object. As a general rule, highly rational writers (like Nabokov) write most comfortably in the morning, and mainly intuitive writers write most comfortably at night. Some writers compose on small cards, one sentence to a card (a crazy way to write, it seems to me, but the method is one some undeniable masters, including Nabokov, have used); and at the opposite extreme some good writers compose on typewriters fed by huge rolls of paper, so that they never have to change a page. Some writers write all day and half the night, never pausing except to keep the body functioning, shifting according to convenience from one writing implement to another, plunging into new scenes late at night when the mind's at its dreamiest, and revising in the morning, when cold-blooded intellect is at its best. Some novelists never write anything but novels, with maybe an occasional journal about a trip; others shift restlessly from form to form—now a play, now a poem, now a short story, now an article about U.S. foreign policy.

Any approach will do. But to any young novelist troubled about how or where he ought to start, I suggest something like the following: If you have trouble with novel-writing, go back for a while to short stories. In a short story it is fairly easy to work out and thus come to understand from within the basic form of storytelling. The genre is small enough that one can grasp the fundamental concepts of fiction—how one event must cause another (however the order of events may be disguised by flashbacks or by odd narrative technique); how characters' motives must be shown dramatically, not just talked about; how setting, character, and action must interpenetrate, each supporting and infusing the others; how plot must have rhythm, so that in some way it builds in intensity toward an emotional high point; how the narrative must have design, a firm structure that gives every part value but does not vulgarly call attention to itself; how style, plot, and meaning must finally be all one.

In writing short stories—as in writing novels—take one thing at a time. (For some writers, this advice I'm giving may apply best to a first draft; for others, it may hinder the flow at first but be useful when time for revision comes.) Treat a short passage of description as a complete unit and make that one small unit as perfect as you can; then turn to the next unit— a passage of dialogue, say—and make that as perfect as you can. Move to larger units, the individual scenes that together make up the plot, and work each scene until it sparkles. Like the stand-up comic who polishes each joke to its highest possible luster (gives each joke its proper accents and timing, proper eye rolls and double takes), polish each element of the total fiction so that the story is not only good as a whole but arresting from moment to moment. As class writing exercises show, almost any writer can write fairly well if he's dealing with one small problem. It's only when the writer gets confused that he begins to sound like an amateur. Break up the larger story into its components, make sure you understand the exact function of each component (a story is like a machine with numerous gears: it should contain no gear that doesn't turn something), and after each component has been carefully set in place, step back and have a look at the whole. Then rewrite until the story flows as naturally as a river, each element so blending with the rest that no one, not even yourself two years from now, can locate the separate parts. (If writing in small units bothers you, don't do it. Some writers are more comfortable pouring out page after page and only then going back to deal with problems; and some, once a draft of the story is down on paper, can rewrite only by going back to the beginning and writing straight through to the end all over again. A terrible way of working, clearly, but all right if it's the only way you've got.) The real message is, write in any way that works for you: write in a tuxedo or in the shower with a raincoat or in a cave deep in the woods.

When you write a novel, start with a plan—a careful plot outline, some notes to yourself on characters and settings, particular important events, and implications of meaning. In my experience, many young writers hate this step; they'd rather just plunge in. That's O.K., up to a point, but sooner or later the writer has no choice but to figure out what he's doing. Consider doing for yourself what movie people call a "treatment," a short narrative telling the whole story, introducing all the characters and events but skipping most of the particulars, including dialogue. Carefully studying and revising the treatment until the story has a clear inevitability, you will find yourself understanding the story's implications more fully than you did with just an outline, and you will save yourself time later. For some writers it may also prove useful to write a detailed critical explication of the text—the text that, so far, exists only in the writer's head. The risk here is obvious: that the resulting novel will be "workshoppy," too neat to move or persuade.

The last step before the actual writing may be the chapter-by-chapter breakdown of the plot. It's here that the writer figures out in detail what information, necessary for understanding later developments, should be worked into Chapter One, what can be slipped into Chapter Three, and so on. Obviously one cannot begin with sixty static pages of exposition setting up the background of the story. Writing a novel is like running grain through a hammer mill: one has to get the central action rolling, and then feed in the background, or sprinkle in the larger implications, whenever and wherever one can do it without losing a finger. For some novels, working in the background is easy; for others, it's torture. In a novel like *Grendel,* all the reader needs to know in order to follow the action is that Grendel is a monster; comes from a cave and from a mute, mindless mother; hates his sense of himself as an animal; and feels mysteriously drawn to human beings, whom he hungrily studies, longs to be friends with, and also scorns and occasionally eats. All this can easily be shown within the first chapter.

On the other hand, working in the background for the action of a novel like *Mickelsson's Ghosts* can drive a writer to the edge of despair. The novel is about a famous philosopher who, midway through his career, suddenly finds himself (as Dante did) lost. He feels he has failed his wife and family (the wife has left him), feels he has betrayed his early promise and the values of his Wisconsin Lutheran background, has lost interest in his students and has ceased to care about philosophical questions, has lost faith and hope in democracy (and owes a large sum of money to the IRS), scorns the university where he teaches and the unsophisticated town in which it's situated, and has good reason to believe he is losing his mind. He cuts himself off from his university community by buying a huge rotting house in the country, which turns out to be haunted (if he can trust his wits), and he finds himself up to the neck in evils he never before dreamt of—middle-of-the-night dumpings of poisonous wastes, witchcraft, backwoods prostitution, a mysterious string of murders, and more. (I need not here run through the whole plot and its conclusion.)

The easy way to write such a novel is to start fairly far back in time, with the breakup of the marriage, say, and then dramatize the philosopher's troubles one by one, in order. The problem is that that is not the real beginning of the story. The real beginning is the moment the philosopher, Peter Mickelsson, chooses to opt out—buy the decaying house in Pennsylvania's Endless Mountains and turn his back on all he formerly believed in or loved. What starts the novel on its dangerous course, in other words, is not Mickelsson's bad luck (that is background information which must somehow be worked in) but Mickelsson's active choice, his quest decision. If the novel is to begin where the story begins, then by the end of Chapter One Mickelsson must at least have located the house he will buy. We must know why he is hunting a house and what the hunt means to him—must understand why he hates living in town near other professors; must know, by the firm proof of dramatized scenes, why he feels superior to those around him; why even very intelligent students annoy him, as do philosophy books and lectures; why he feels himself a failure (what his family was like, what his career was like earlier, what kind of house he lived in in his days in the Ivy League); and we must understand why he's afraid he's going mad (we must see in action what it is that deeply disturbs him), and we must already in this chapter have the opportunity to observe (not just hear about from the narrator) the streak of violence in Mickelsson that enables him to cut himself off from those around him— a streak that will, later in the novel, enable him to behave in even less admirable ways—and all this must be shown without undermining Mickelsson's credibility as a brilliant man, someone who really might once have been an Ivy League professor of philosophy.

Though I knew from the beginning (more or less) the nature of the problems facing me, I cannot say I figured out the answers intellectually. I knew that, within the span of the first of the thirty- to forty-page chapters my plan of the novel allowed me (long chapters for a dense, elephantine rhythm), I could not hope to do more than introduce Mickelsson's main troubles, bringing each forward in sharp relief, then leaving its development to later chapters, wherever I could work the material in; and I knew that I would have to find a few strong scenes, sufficiently slow-moving (though dramatic and active) to allow maximum drift to Mickelsson's mind. I knew that for power, or emotional energy, I would have to depend on the force of Mickelsson's character—fuming, repressed rage and self-doubt, a deep nastiness barely reined in, and a sentimental streak always on the verge of turning repellent, saved at the last moment by Mickelsson's intelligence, the backlash of irony—a character force I would have to support by the best prose (or at least the most difficult to achieve) I'd ever written: huge, rolling sentences as dense and crackling as my weight-lifter, former-college-football-star, mad philosopher.

It depresses me to think how many versions I wrote of this first chapter and the two that followed it—working on these three in a block because they laid out all the main themes and background events to be developed, as well as, of course, advancing the present action. (By the end of the third chapter Mickelsson knows that, according to his mountain neighbors, his house is haunted.) Getting the hundred-page, three-chapter block finally right took more than a year of steady writing and revising and saw one dramatic scene after another invented, frantically polished, then discarded. In the end I settled for: (1) A large scene in which Mickelsson fumes and sweats in his overheated third-floor apartment, then walks the night streets, looking enviously at other people's large houses and imagining the lives inside, comparing them with his own lost life, hating these mediocre professors (as he thinks them) whose luck has turned out to be so much better than his own—a scene that ends with Mickelsson's killing a large black dog that threatens him on the sidewalk. (2) A scene at the university, where Mickelsson's department chairman, whom he hates, wangles out of him an undergraduate advising job (not one of Mickelsson's responsibilities) for an unpleasant young man who wants to transfer to philosophy from engineering. (3) A scene presenting Mickelsson's angry decision to look for a house in the country, then his search, concluding with his finding the ancient and eerie house in the mountains. Developed in detail, allowing space for Mickelsson's memories and ironic internal observations, this arrangement of scenes finally satisfied me, insofar as one can ever be satisfied in these matters. Together they move the story forward by a direct chain of cause and effect. The climax of the first scene, Mickelsson's killing of the dog, frightens him and gives focus to his paranoia (specifically his fear that people like his chairman are watching and judging him, suspecting the failure of which he accuses himself). The climax of the second scene, in which the unpleasant engineering student insists on enrolling in Mickelsson's own course, tips the scales of Mickelsson's increasing inclination to move as far as he can from the university without giving up his job completely. And within these sprawling scenes it is possible to place directly before the reader, in dialogue and action (sometimes in momentary flashback), the main forces that have brought Mickelsson to this moment.

As I've said, I didn't work all this out intellectually. I worked out *a* plan, did my best with it, revised it, and finally discarded it. I worked out another, and then others after that, and by muddling along, sometimes reclaiming an element or two from a scrapped approach, I finally came up with something that would do, at least for me. Except in extremely simple novels—novels almost not worth writing, in my opinion—the most careful plan in the world won't actually work. Things intended for one chapter turn out to take two, and since the overall rhythm of the novel will not allow the division, one has to overhaul the whole scheme. But an inadequate plan is better than none. Writing a novel is like heading out over the open sea in a small boat. If you have a plan and a course laid out, that's helpful. If you drift off course, checking the stars can help you find a new course. If you have no map, no course laid out, sooner or later confusion will make you check the stars.

When the tentative plan is done, maybe scrawled almost illegibly in a fat, shedding notebook, maybe tacked up neatly around the walls of your room, on butcher paper, you're ready to start the writing—if you haven't started already, turning back to the planning stage only when driven by desperation. If you have prepared yourself well, there is nothing more anyone need tell you. If you have taken the time to learn to write beautiful, rock-firm sentences, if you have mastered evocation of the vivid and continuous dream, if you are generous enough in your personal character to treat imaginary characters and readers fairly, if you have held on to your childhood virtues and have not settled for literary standards much lower than those of the fiction you admire, then the novel you write will eventually be, after the necessary labor of repeated revision, a novel to be proud of, one that almost certainly someone, sooner or later, will be glad to publish. (It may be that you can only get it published after other, later novels have proved successful.) If you do none of the things I advise in this book, then you may nevertheless, by some freak of fortune or grace, write a novel to be proud of. (The god of novelists will not be tyrannized by rules.) If, on the other hand, you miserably fail, you have only three choices: start over, or start something else, or quit.

Finally, the true novelist is the one who doesn't quit. Novel-writing is not so much a profession as a *yoga*, or "way," an alternative to ordinary life-in-the-world. Its benefits are quasi-religious—a changed quality of mind and heart, satisfactions no non-novelist can understand—and its rigors generally bring no profit except to the spirit. For those who are authentically called to the profession, spiritual profits are enough.

INDEX